PREFAB. How many modules do you need to live?
Copyright © 2017 Instituto Monsa de ediciones

Editor, concept, and project director
Anna Minguet

Project's selection, design and layout
Patricia Martínez (equipo editorial Monsa)

INSTITUTO MONSA DE EDICIONES
Gravina 43 (08930)
Sant Adrià de Besòs
Barcelona (Spain)
Tlf. +34 93 381 00 50
www.monsa.com
monsa@monsa.com

Visit our official online store!
www.monsashop.com

Follow us!
Facebook: @monsashop
Instagram: @monsapublications

Cover images © 2by4-architects (Island House)

ISBN: 978-84-16500-61-1
D.L. B 23410-2017
Printed by Impuls 45

PREFAB

How many modules do you need to live?

monsa

INTRODUCTION

How many modules do you need to live?
With this simple question we present this new book about prefabricated and modular construction. Showing options for expanding or downsizing according to each person's need for space, and the ease with which you can move the home to a new place.

The company has made use of prefabrication and industrial methods by moving the building's construction processes to factories or workshops in which frames, modules, panels and assembly kits are manufactured.

The history of prefabricated architecture is an exciting journey through the desires and needs of individuals and the societies in which they live. Industrial processes create products and goods for society in order to meet its needs, achieving sustainable, contemporary, quality architecture.

We have presented projects arranged in order from less to more, from constructions comprised of just 1 module to others that are made up of 11, homes that are economical, green, and durable.

¿Cuántos módulos necesitas para vivir?
Con esta simple pregunta presentamos este nuevo libro de construcciones prefabricadas y modulares. Mostrando opciones para ampliar o disminuir según las necesidades de espacio de cada persona, y la facilidad de poder transportar el hogar a una nueva zona.

La sociedad se ha valido de la prefabricación y de los métodos industrializados trasladando los procesos constructivos del propio emplazamiento del edificio a fábricas o talleres en los que se fabrican marcos, bastidores, módulos, paneles y kits de montaje.

La historia de la arquitectura prefabricada es un apasionante recorrido por los deseos y necesidades de los individuos y de las sociedades en las que viven. Los procesos industriales crean productos y bienes para la sociedad con el fin de satisfacer las necesidades de la misma, consiguiendo una arquitectura de calidad, sostenible y contemporánea.

Hemos presentado los proyectos ordenados de menos a más, desde construcciones de sólo 1 módulo hasta otras de 11, hogares económicos, ecológicos y duraderos.

DESERT ZEN RETRETA
Modules: 1, 2 or 3 Boxes

House Port
Location: Desert Hot Springs, CA, USA
Photos © Avery Meyers

The ingenious central idea of this project is hidden behind its minimalist lines. These homes are composed of prefabricated modules (one, two or three of them depending on the owner's needs), which share a roof but are not joined together, thus just 2100 sq ft of the total 5400 sq ft is behind walls. The property is not bound to its surroundings; it is a part of their very essence.

La idea central de este proyecto esconde su genialidad tras el minimalismo de sus líneas. Una vivienda compuesta por módulos prefabricados (uno, dos o tres según las necesidades del propietario) que comparten techo pero no están unidos entre si. De esta forma, de los 500 m² de la vivienda, solo 195 están entre paredes. La vivienda no se une al entorno; el entorno es parte de su esencia.

The modules are made of SIP panels and the roof of galvanised metal. Both materials provide the house with great heat and sound insulation.

Los módulos están compuestos de paneles SIP, y el tejado de metal galvanizado. Ambos materiales proporcionan un gran aislamiento térmico y acústico a la casa.

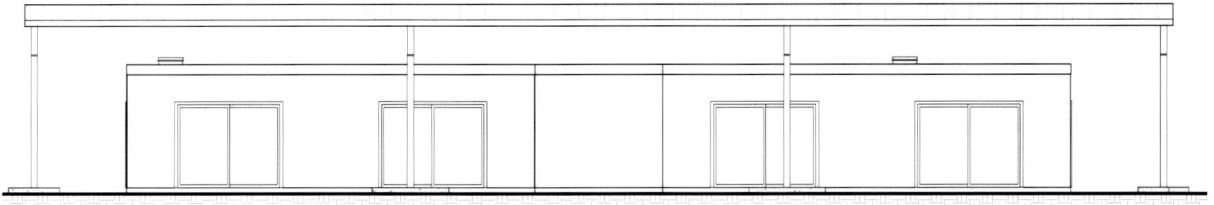

Front elevation

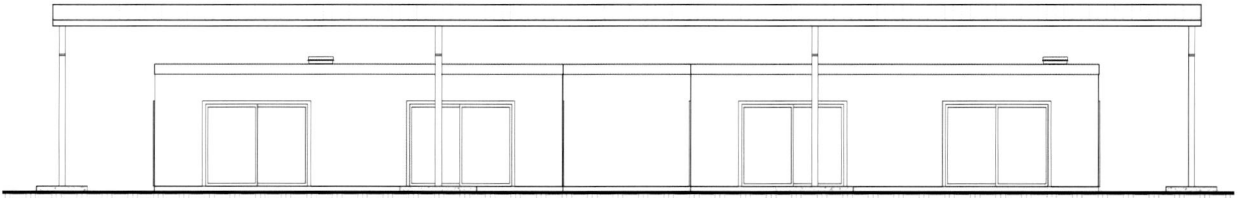

Back elevation

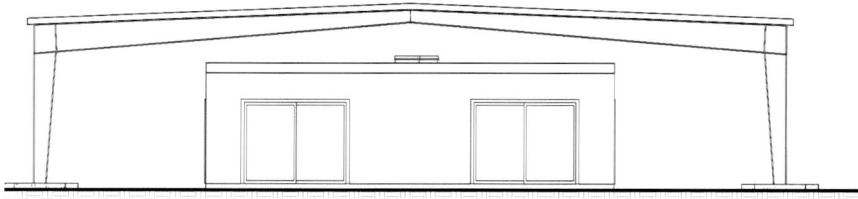

Right side elevation

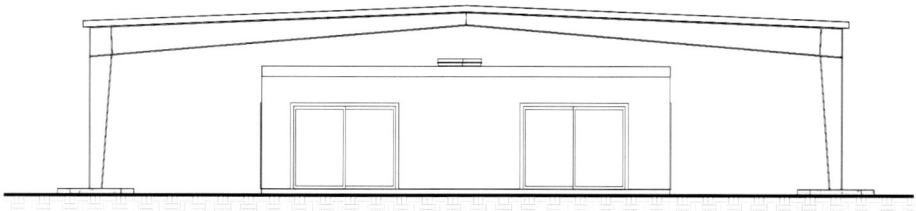

Left side elevation

Within the modules the rooms are spacious and very bright, with huge windows that draw the exterior environment right into the house.

Dentro de los módulos, las habitaciones son amplias y muy luminosas, con grandes ventanales que acercan la zona exterior de la vivienda a la interior.

Beach style interior perspective

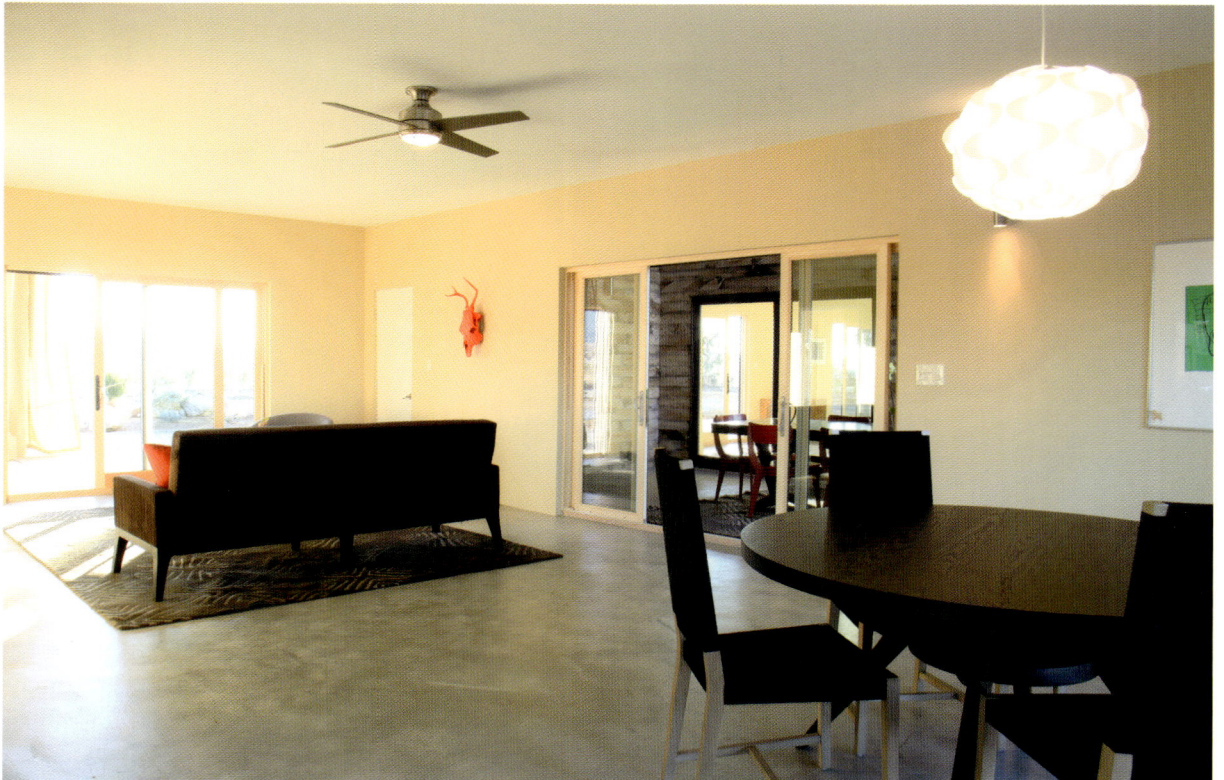

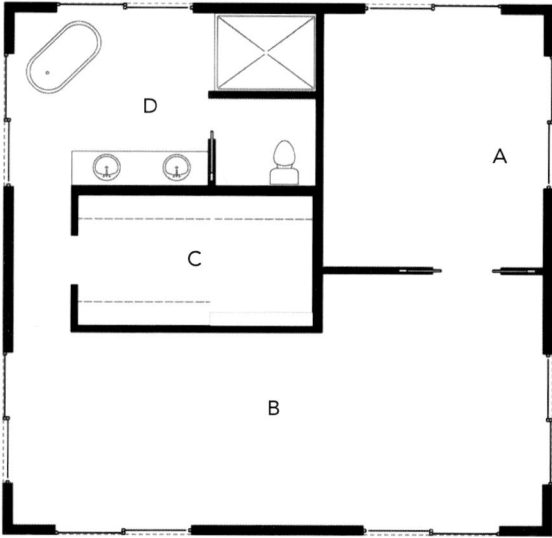

Master suite configuration

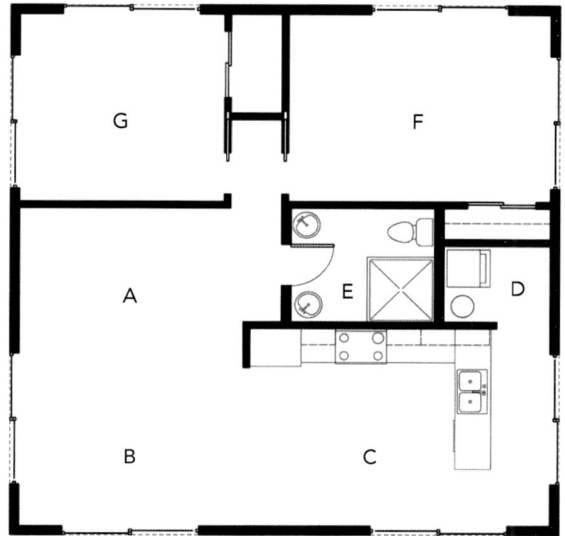

A. Master sitting room
B. Master bedroom
C. Walk-in-closet
D. Master bathroom

Double bedroom configuration

A. Great room
B. Dining area
C. Kitchen
D. Laundry room
E. Bathroom
F. Bedroom
G. Guest bedroom/
   Office

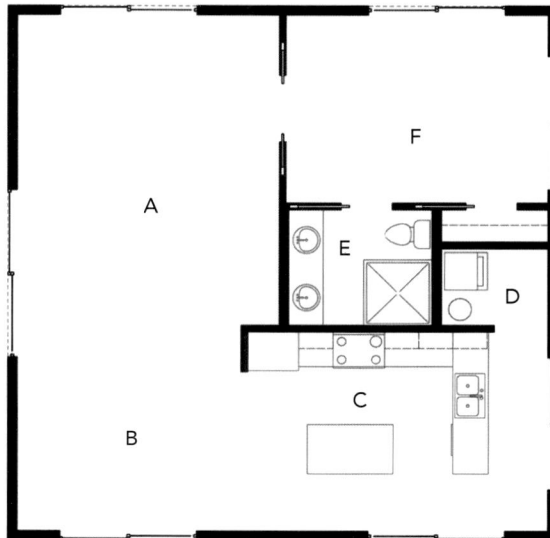

Single bedroom configuration

A. Great room
B. Dining room
C. Kitchen
D. Laundry room
E. Bathroom
F. Guestroom/Studio

ISLAND HOUSE
Modules: 1 Box

2by4-architects
Location: Loosdrechtse, The Netherlands
Photos © 2by4-architects

This house was not originally conceived as a prefab, but its growing popularity let the design team to create a prefab version. The new design is more affordable and faster to build, while at the same time, it maintains the features of the original design. Its flexible design makes it suitable for a wide range of uses.

En su origen no era una casa prefabricada pero, conforme creció su popularidad, el equipo de arquitectura decidió crear una versión que sí lo fuera. Este nuevo diseño reduce tanto costes como tiempo de construcción y, al mismo tiempo, conserva las características del original. Un diseño flexible que permite una gran variedad de usos.

Photomontage

Wall cabinet. Closed

Located on an island in the Dutch lake area "Loosdrechtse Plassen" the house is accessed through a jetty.

Ubicada en una isla de la zona de lagos holandesa Loosdrechtse Plassen, se accede a la vivienda por un embarcadero.

Wall cabinet. Open

A set of glass sliding doors that lead to a deck and a wood façade that can be folded away maximize the connection with the natural setting.

La conexión con el entorno es máxima, gracias a las puertas correderas de cristal que conducen al puerto y a la fachada de madera plegable.

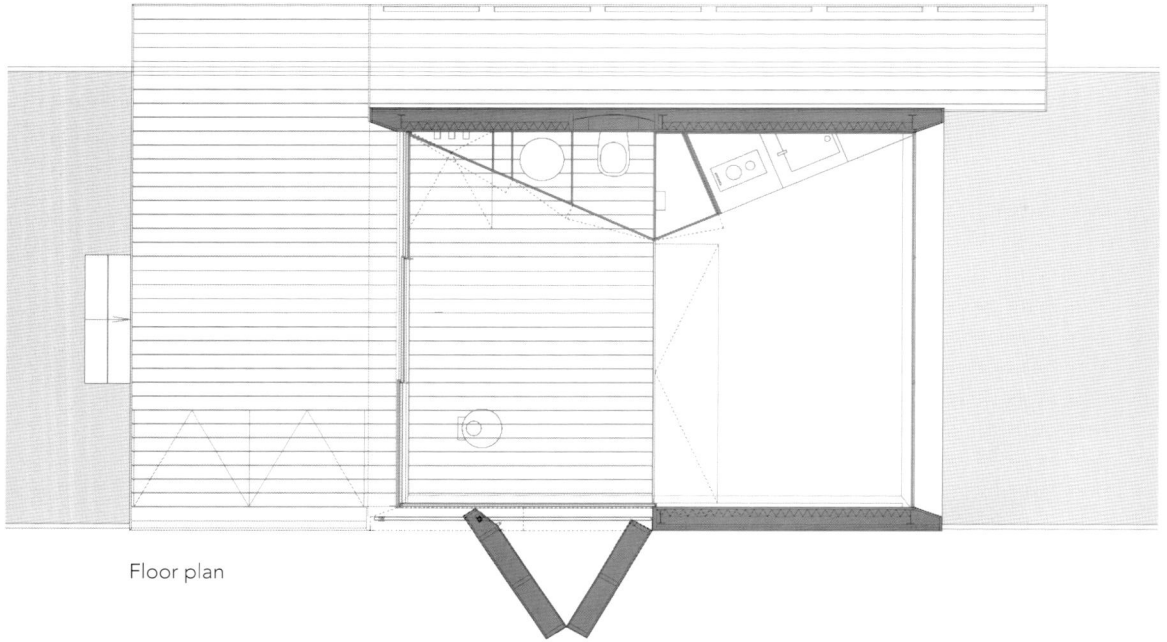
Floor plan

Sketch

Section

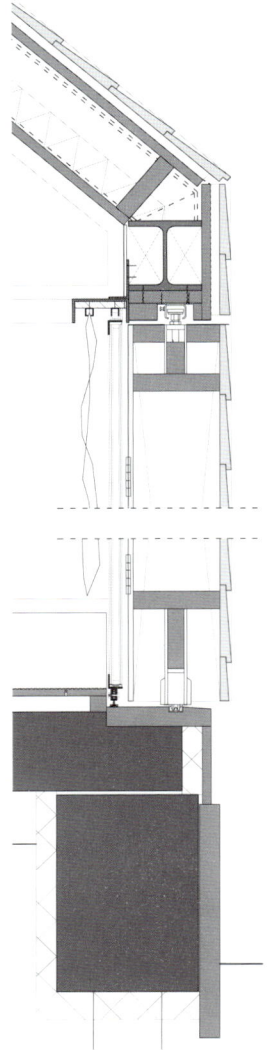

Wall section detail

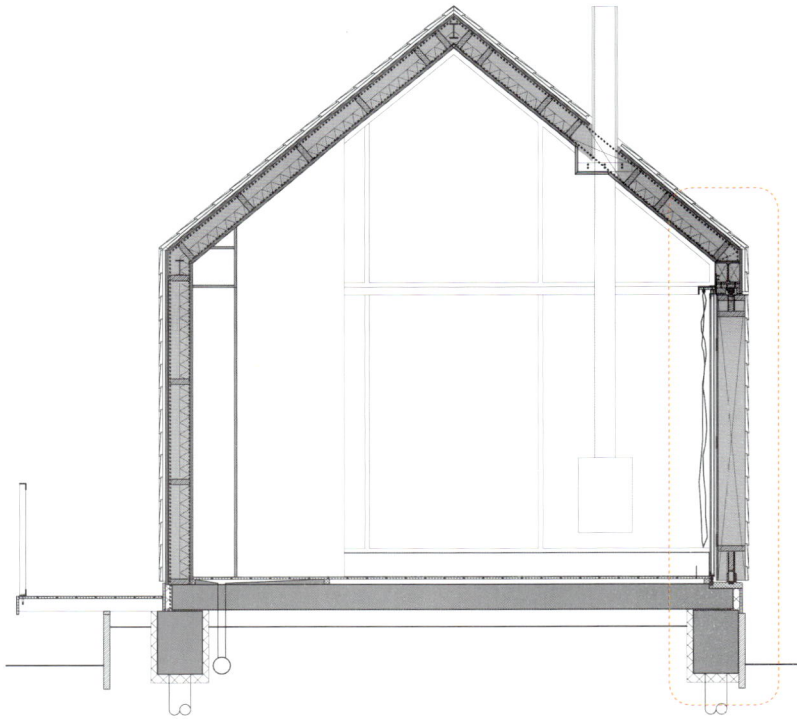

Although the size of the house is limited, it satisfies all the needs of a household with a bathroom and integrated in a built-in wall unit.

El espacio está muy limitado, pero el diseño incluye un módulo con baño para poder cumplir con todas las funciones del hogar.

32nd STREET MODULAR

Modules: 2 Boxes

Tomecek Studio
Location: Denver, CO, USA
Photos © Tomecek Studio

"I wanted to experiment with my own home to see if it was possible to create a modern, environmentally friendly design using a prefabricated modular system." This architect has pushed the customisation of modular designs to its absolute limit without losing the benefits. "It cuts build time and materials wastage to just 5%", he states, highly satisfied.

"Quería probar en mi propia casa si podía conseguir un diseño moderno y ecológico con un sistema modular prefabricado." Así presenta el arquitecto este proyecto, que llevó al límite las posibilidades de personalización de los diseños modulares sin perder sus ventajas. "Se reduce el tiempo de edificación y la pérdida de material hasta solo un 5%", afirma satisfecho.

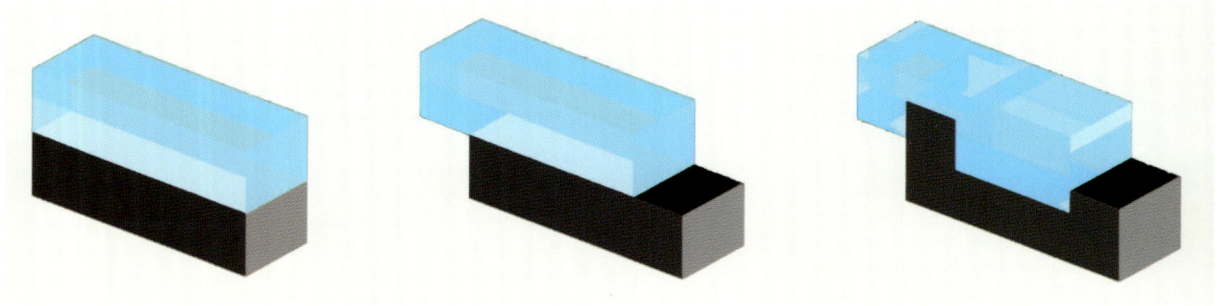

Massing diagrams

80% of the house was created in the workshop. "It took just five hours to lay the foundations and erect the entire structure of the house," says the owner.

El 80% de la casa se hizo en el taller. "Solo llevó 5 horas realizar la cimentación y levantar la estructura completa de la casa", afirma el propietario.

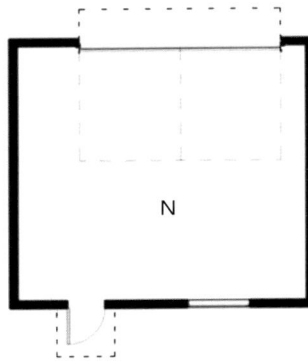

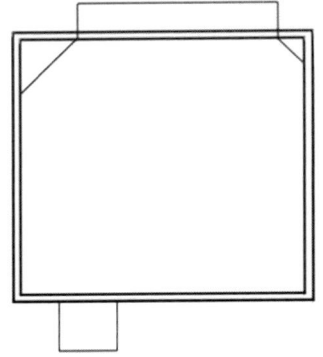

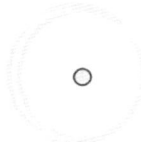

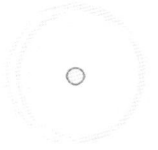

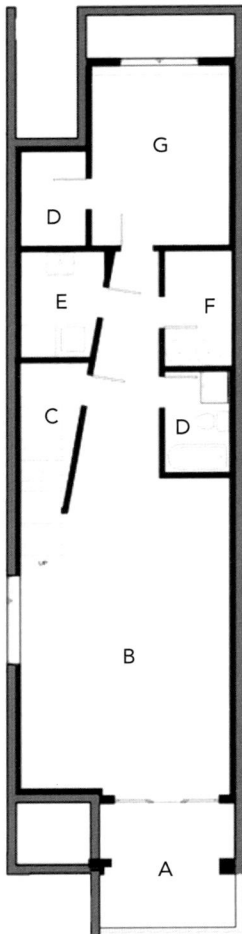

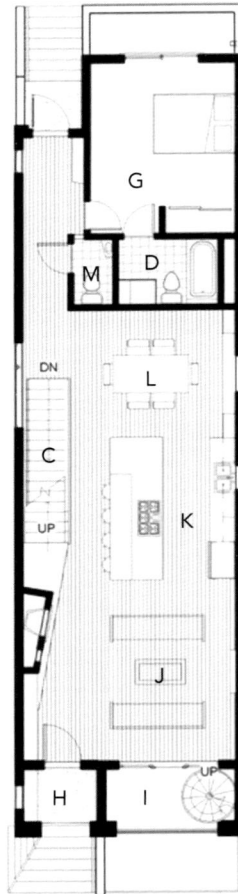

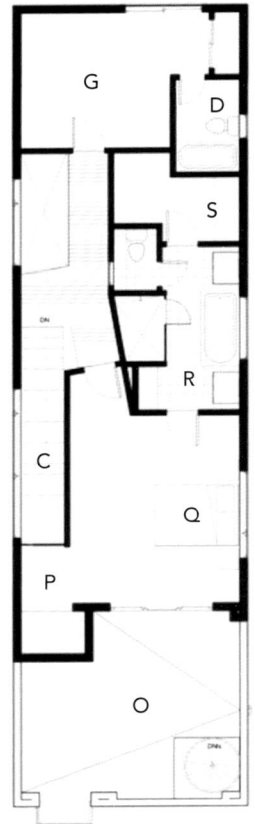

Lower main floor

Main floor plan

Upper floor plan

Two modules are positioned, moved off centre, and then anchored together, creating a terrace to the south and a covered rear entrance to the north.

El origen son dos módulos superpuestos, desfasados y posteriormente anclados entre sí, que dan lugar a una terraza al sur y una entrada trasera cubierta, al norte.

G. Garden
H. Family room
 I. Stair
J. Bathroom
K. Laundry room
L. Mechanical room
M. Bedroom
N. Entry
O. Deck
P. Living area
Q. Kitchen
R. Dining room
S. Powder room
T. Garage
U. Deck
V. Sitting area/Library
W. Master bedroom
X. Master bathroom
Y. Master closet

UNIMOG HOUSE
Modules: 2 Boxes

Fabian Evers Architecture and Wezel Architektur
Location: Ammerbuch, Germany
Photos © Michael Schnabel, Sebastian Berger

A huge challenge: to build a combined home and workshop on a very tight budget on a busy street, surrounded by houses and farms. It was achieved by using two overlapping modules with different finishes in order to separate the two areas. The end result is an unconventional building that makes the most of its resources to ensure the comfort of its inhabitants.

Un desafío de gran potencial: construir con un presupuesto muy ajustado una vivienda-taller, junto a una calle con mucho tráfico y rodeada de casas y granjas. Se resolvió mediante el uso de dos módulos superpuestos, con distintos acabados para separar tareas. El resultado final es una edificación poco convencional que aprovecha al máximo sus recursos para el confort de sus habitantes.

Section

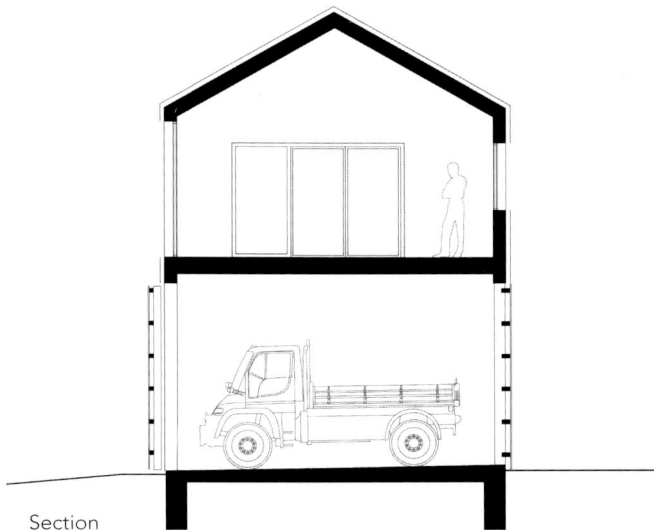

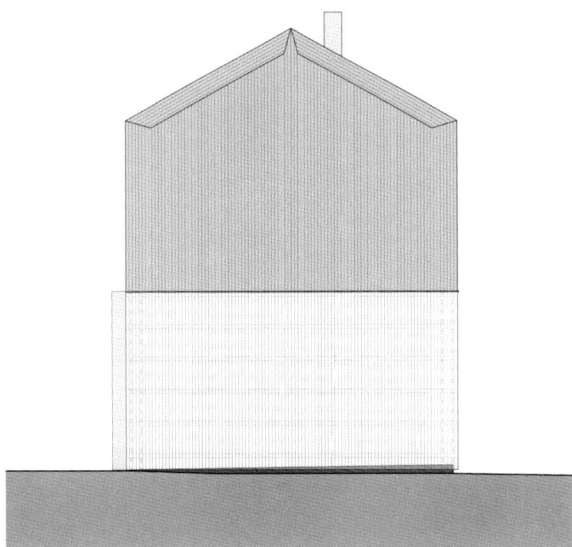

East elevation

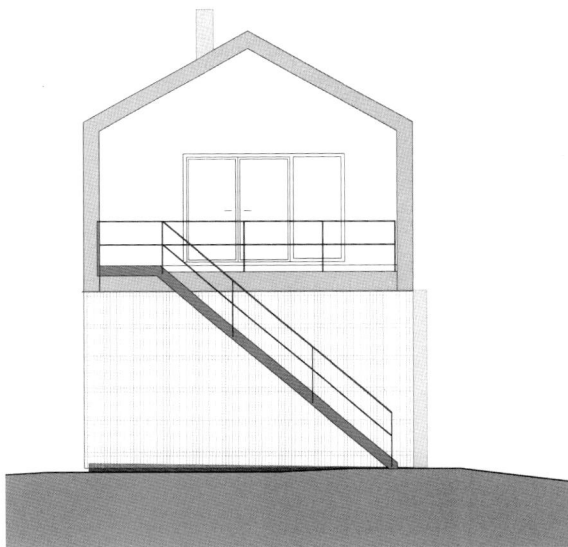

West elevation

The ground-floor workshop frontage is is made of translucent polycarbonate panels that allow sunlight in during the day while blocking it out at night.

La fachada del taller en la planta baja está hecha con paneles de policarbonato traslúcido, que deja pasar la luz solar durante el día y la desprende por la noche.

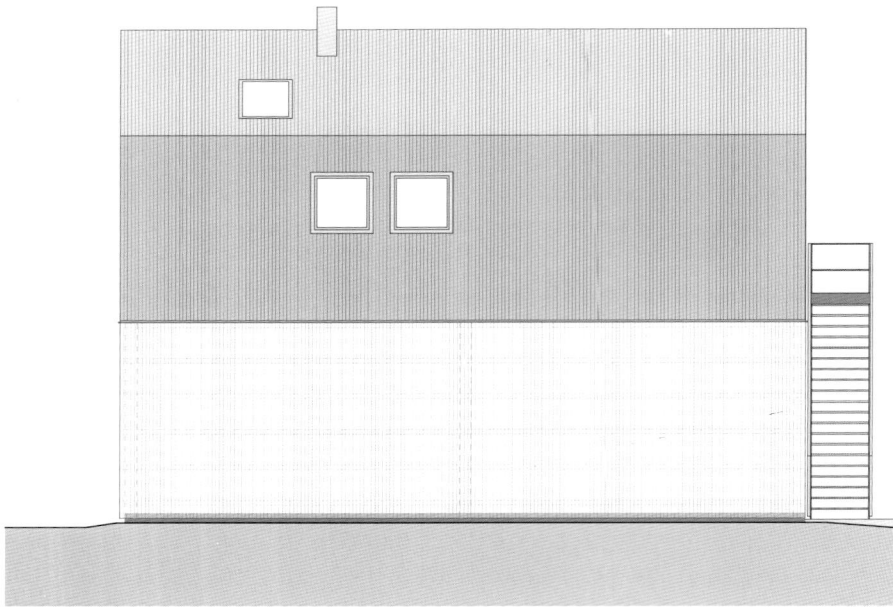

North elevation

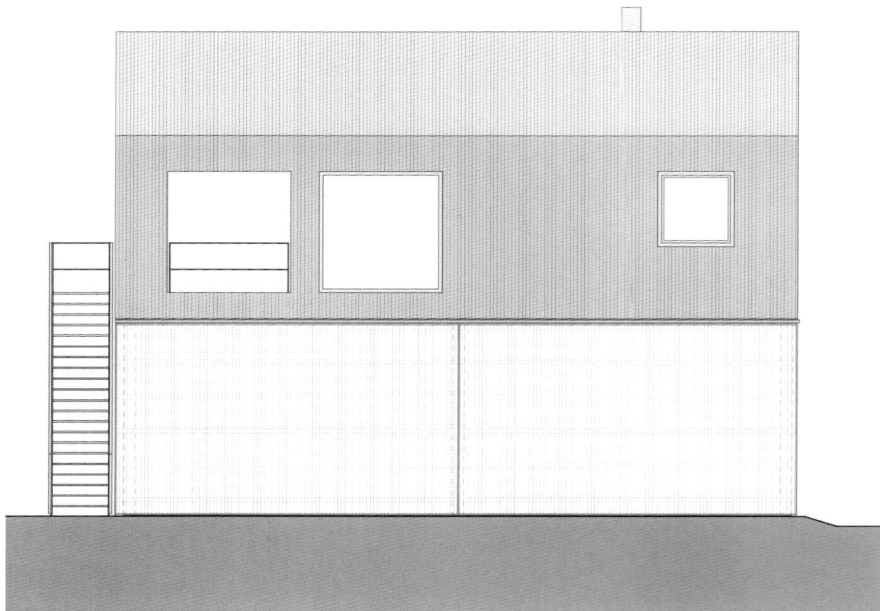

South elevation

a

A

B

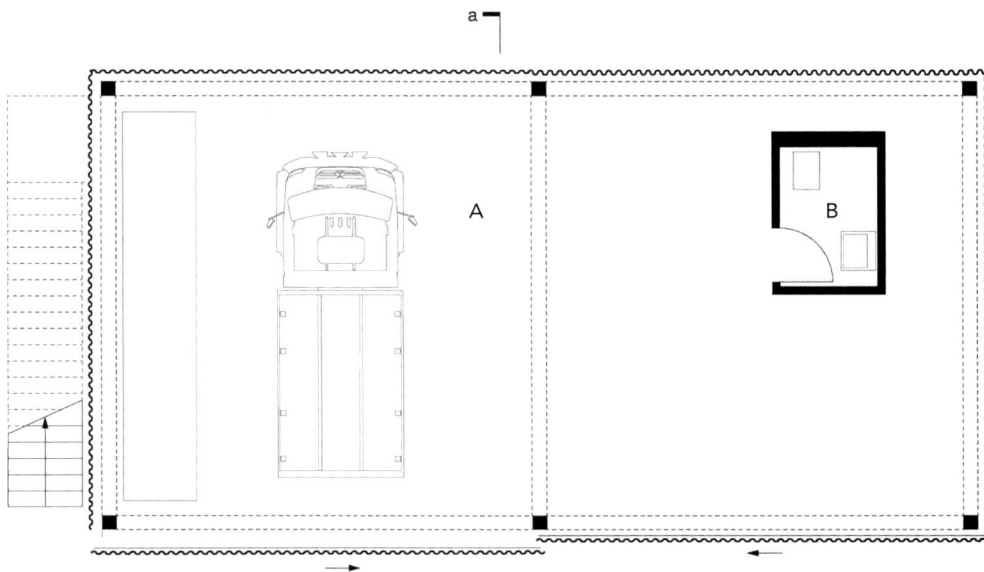

Ground floor plan

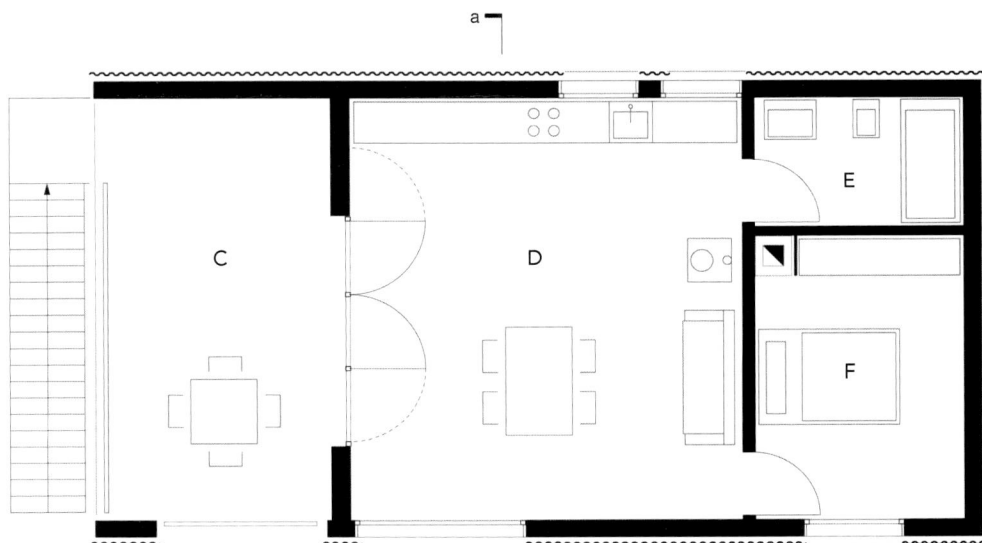

a

a

C

D

E

F

Second floor plan

a

0   1   5

A. Workshop
B. Toilet
C. Porch
D. Living / Dining / Kitchen
E. Bathroom
F. Bedroom

BRONX BOX

Modules: 2 Boxes

Resolution: 4 Architecture. Joseph Tanney, Robert Luntz
Location: Bronx, New York City, USA
Photos © RES4

The house is clad in cement board with Ipe wood decks to keep maintenance issues at a minimum and to reflect similar colours and textures of the neighbourhood. The Bronx Box takes advantage of the efficiencies of off-site construction, holds itself to LEED for Homes standards and has been accepted as another unique personality in its Bronx neighbourhood.

La vivienda está revestida con tablones de cemento y madera de Ipé para reducir al mínimo el mantenimiento y reflejar de una manera similar los colores y texturas del vecindario. La Bronx Box saca provecho de la eficacia de la construcción en fábrica, respeta el sistema de certificación LEED (Liderazgo en Diseño de Energía y Medio Ambiente) de viviendas y ha sido bien aceptada por su personalidad única en el vecindario del Bronx.

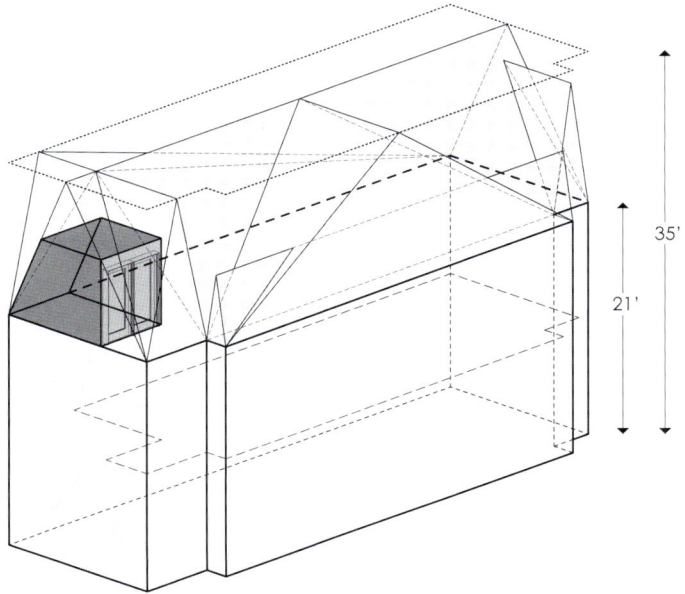

Allowable building envelope   Stair bulkhead

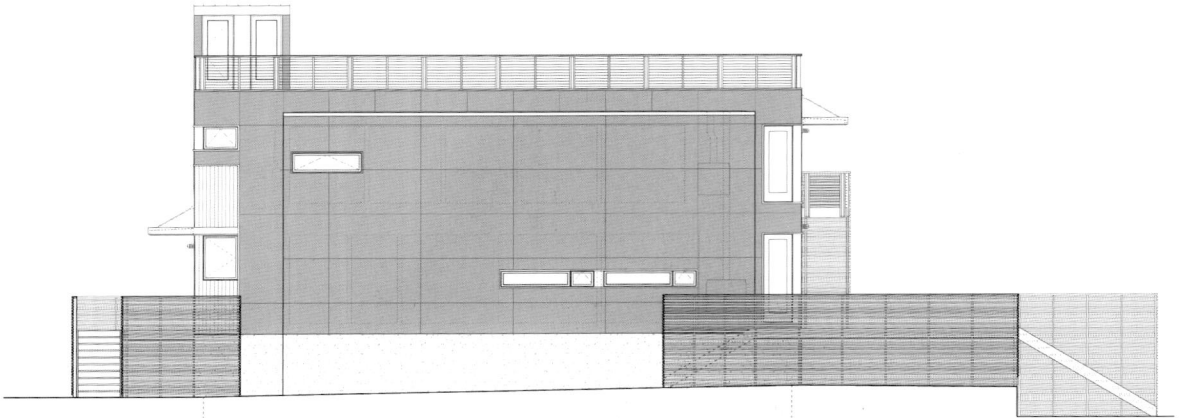

South elevation

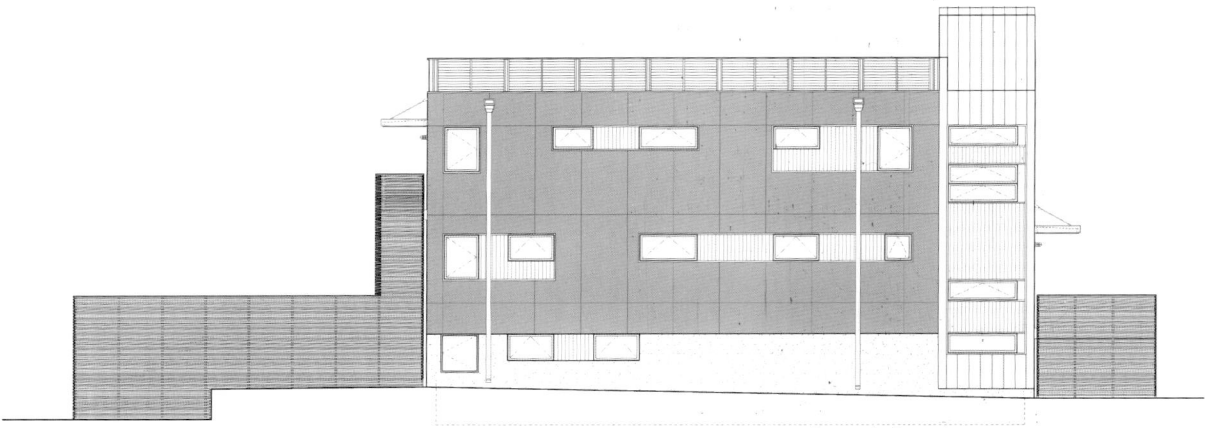

North elevation

The Single Bar Series provides the most economical and efficient solution within the Modern Modular line of prefabricated homes. Within a compact single unit, the home contains two well-sized bedrooms with ample storage space. Through use of an inverted pitched roof, the bar opens to its surroundings, providing natural light throughout the house.

La serie Single Bar (un módulo) ofrece la solución más económica y eficaz dentro de la línea Modern Modular de casas prefabricadas. Con una unidad individual compacta, la vivienda contiene dos dormitorios de buen tamaño con amplio espacio de almacenamiento. Mediante un tejado a dos aguas invertido, el módulo se abre al entorno, proporcionando luz natural a toda la casa.

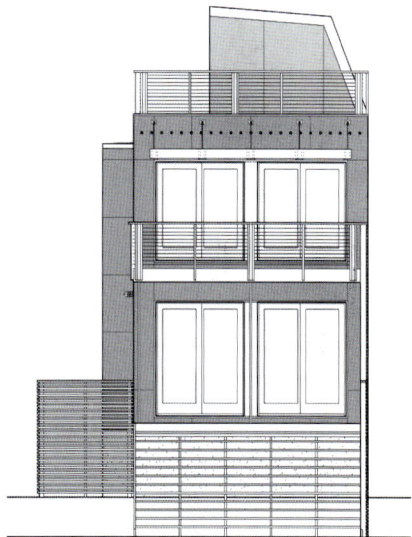

West elevation

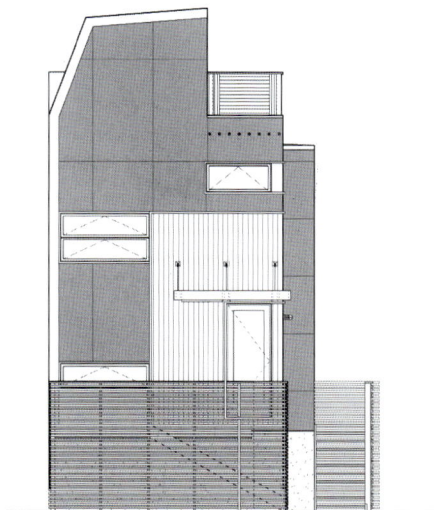

East elevation

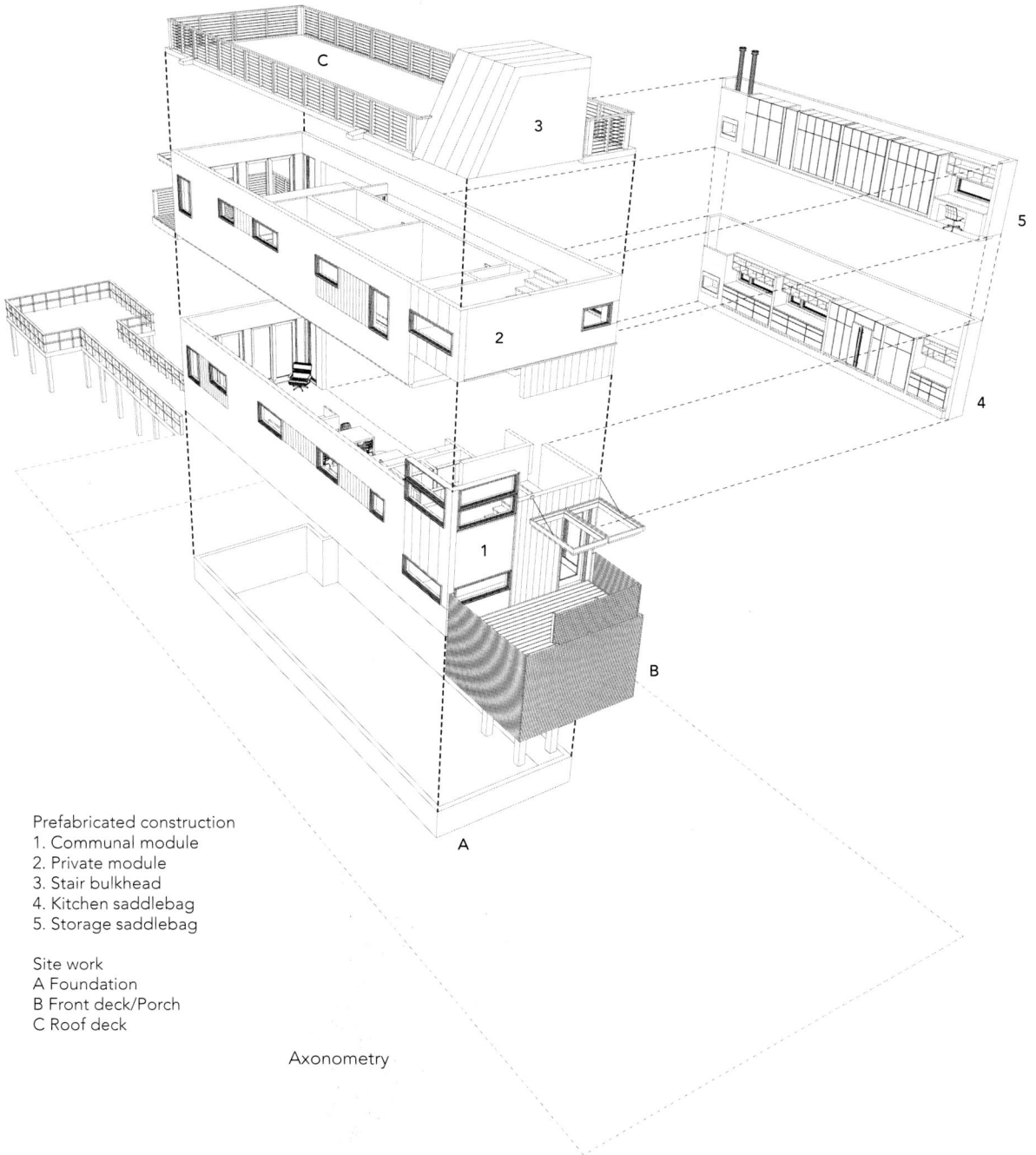

C

3

2

5

4

1

B

A

Prefabricated construction
1. Communal module
2. Private module
3. Stair bulkhead
4. Kitchen saddlebag
5. Storage saddlebag

Site work
A Foundation
B Front deck/Porch
C Roof deck

Axonometry

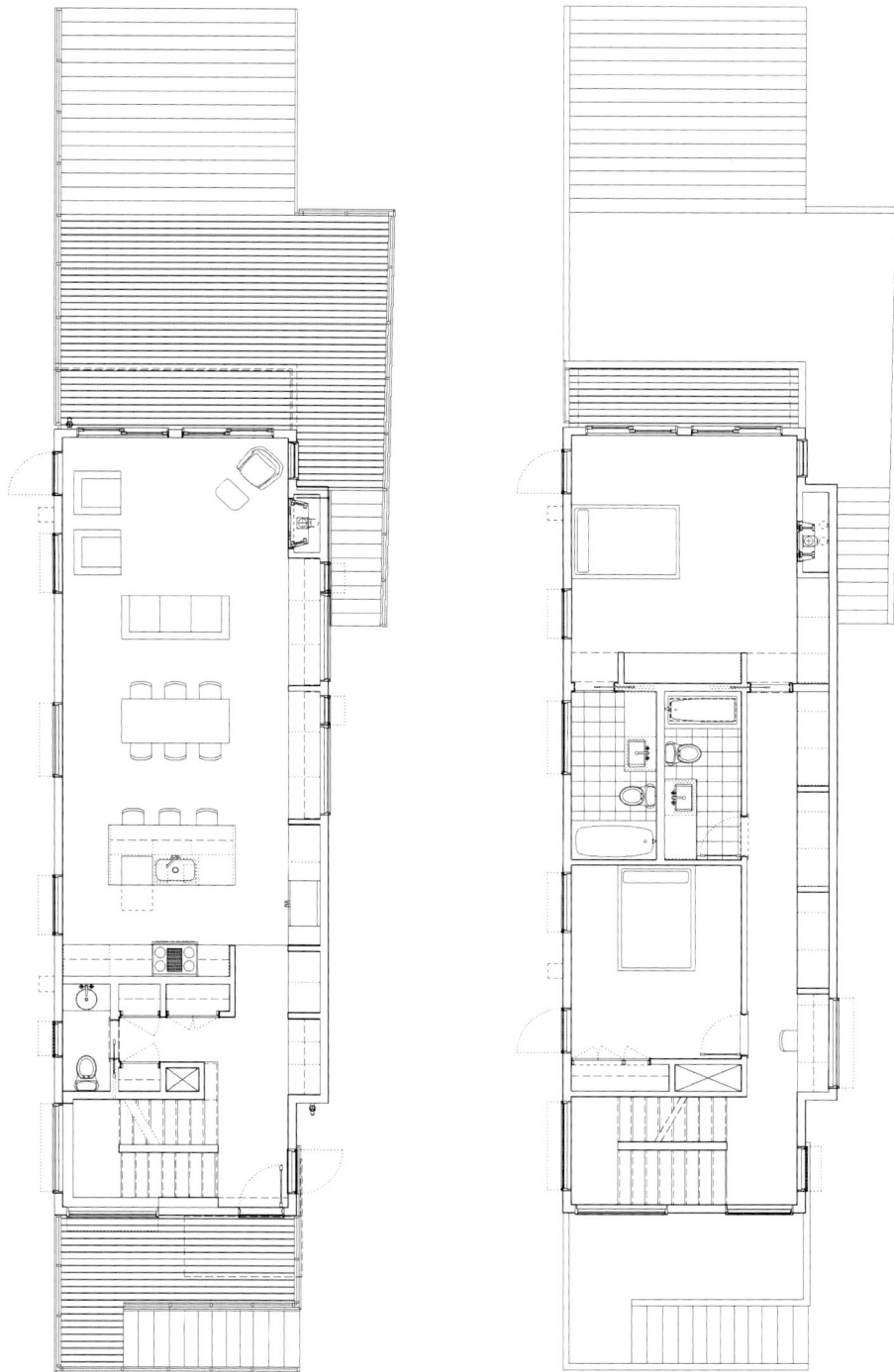

Floor plans

B-LINE MEDIUM 002
Modules: 3 Boxes

Hive Modular
Location: Saint Paul, MN, USA
Photos © Hive Modular, Dave Schmit

David Schmit wanted a detached house with large open spaces and a distinct loft-design feel. Furthermore, the house needed to comply with strict stylistic requirements due to its location in a designated area of historic importance. The solution was a B-line prefabricated home that can be built according to the owner's individual taste and the size of the particular plot.

David Schmit quería una casa unifamiliar que contase con grandes espacios abiertos y recordase a un *loft*. Además, la vivienda debía cumplir unos requisitos estilísticos estrictos, por encontrarse en un barrio histórico. La solución fue una vivienda prefabricada B-line, que permite construir casas adaptadas al gusto del propietario y a las dimensiones de la finca.

North elevation

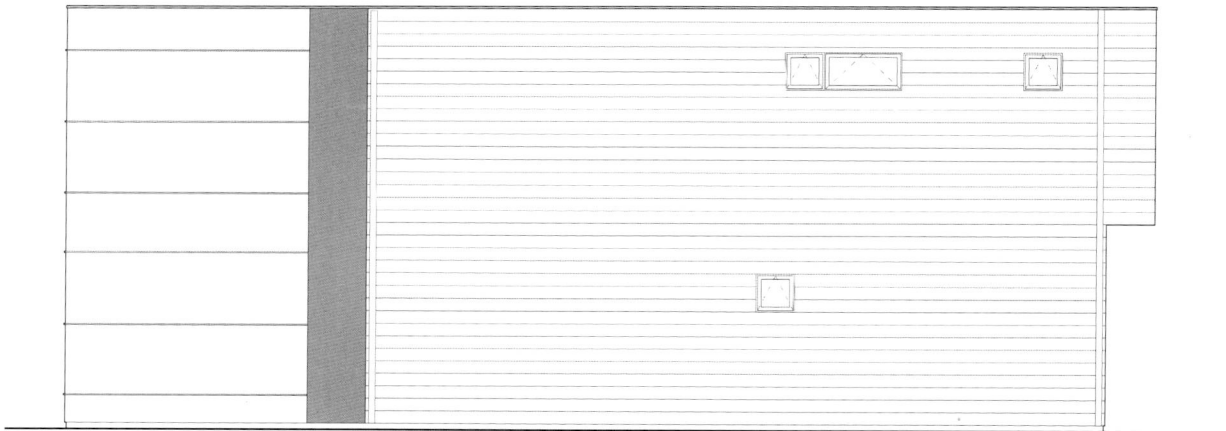

South elevation

The construction is based on a union of three modules. The first encompasses the living room, the second the kitchen and entrance, and the third the upper floor.

La construcción se basa en la unión de tres módulos: el primero cubre el salón-comedor, el segundo la cocina y entrada y el tercero compone la primera planta.

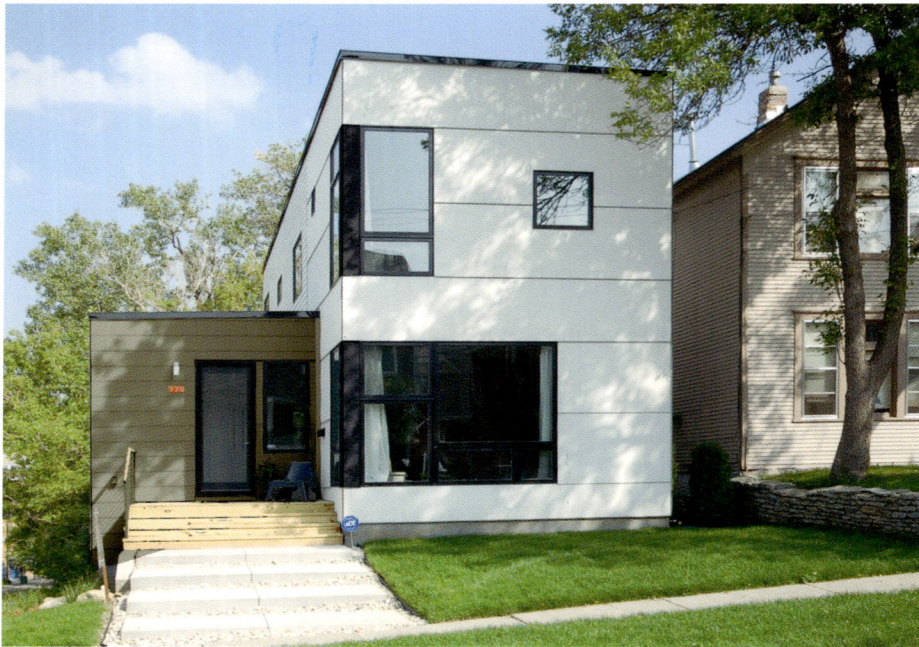

East elevation

West elevation

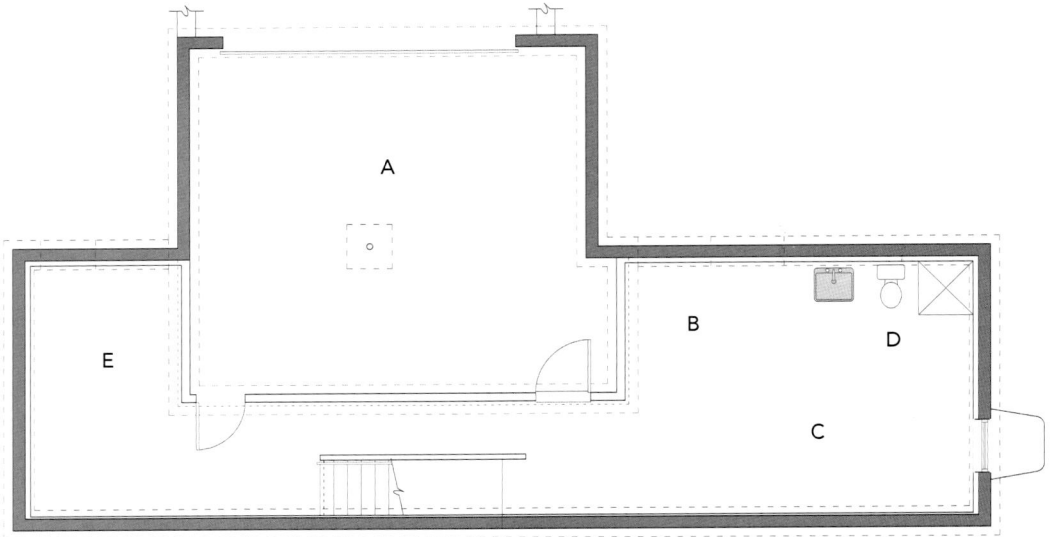

Basement floor plan

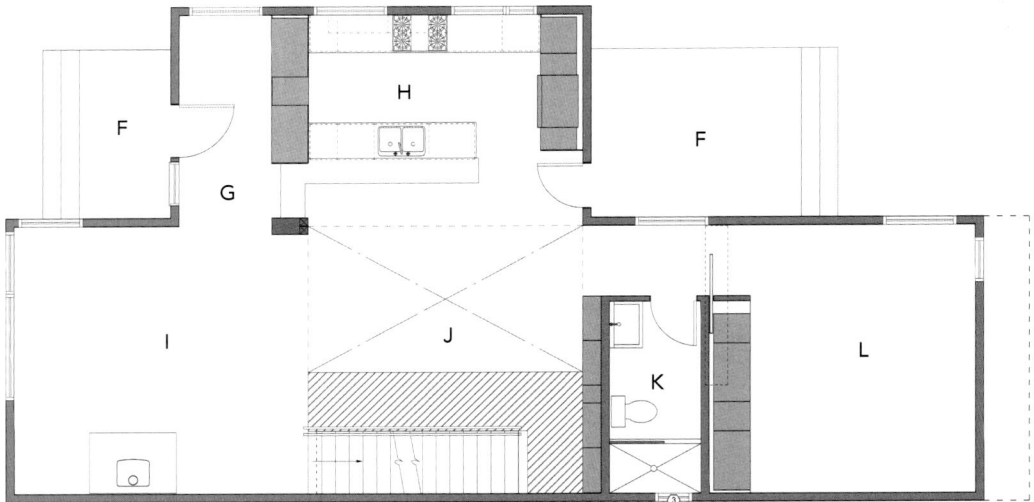

Ground floor plan

Once all the building permissions were in place, the actual construction of the home lasted just a single morning. The 2,020 sq ft house has two floors and an underground garage.

Ya con todos los permisos arquitectónicos para la construcción, la edificación duró una mañana. La casa de 188 m² consta de dos plantas y garaje subterráneo.

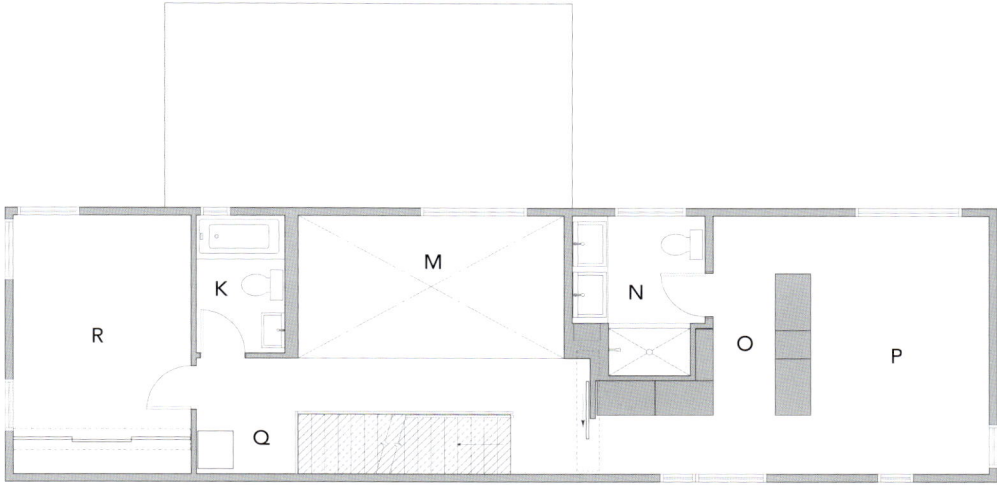

Second floor plan

A. Two-car garage
B. Mechanical
C. Storage
D. Bath rough-ins
E. Mud room
F. Deck
G. Entry
H. Kitchen
I. Living room
J. Dining room
K. Bathroom
L. Study / Guest bedroom
M. Open to below
N. Master bathroom
O. Master closet
P. Master bedroom
Q. Laundry room
R. Bedroom

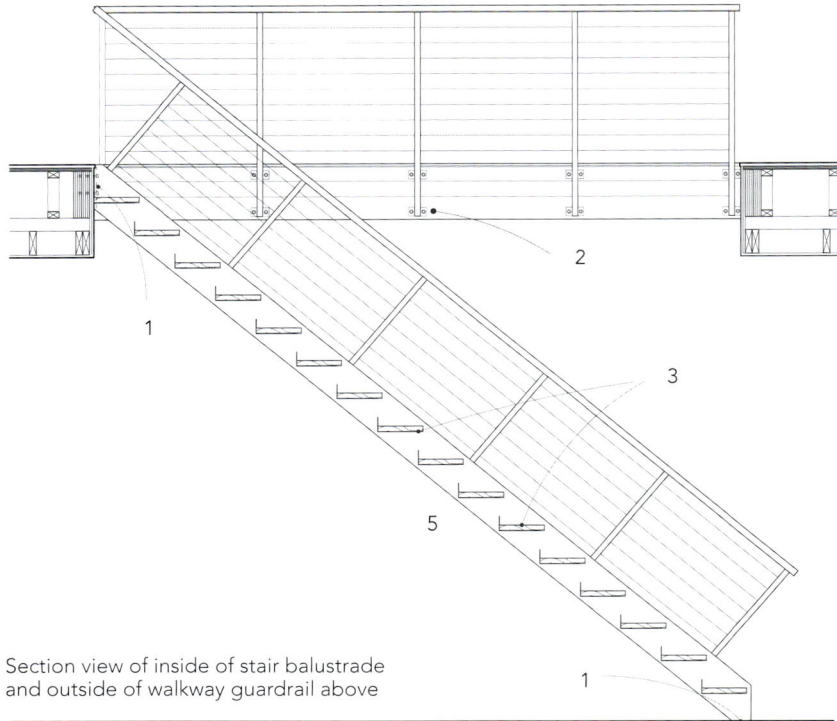

Section view of inside of stair balustrade
and outside of walkway guardrail above

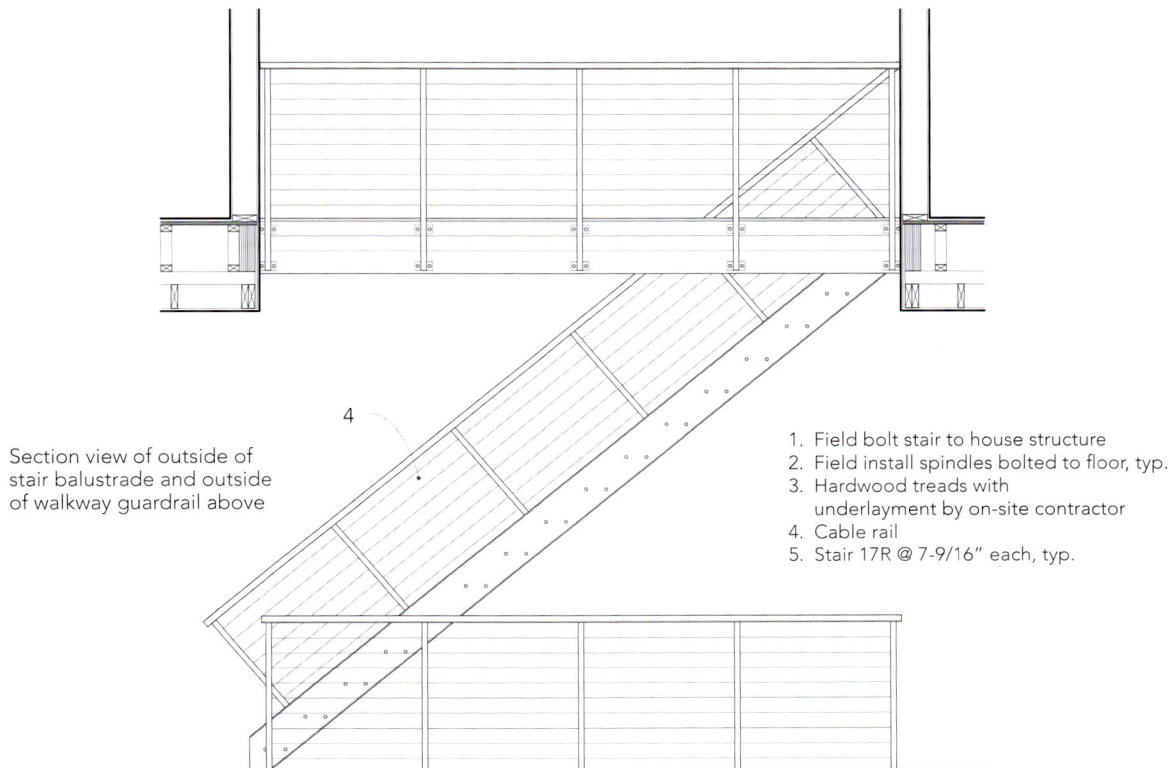

Section view of outside of
stair balustrade and outside
of walkway guardrail above

4

1. Field bolt stair to house structure
2. Field install spindles bolted to floor, typ.
3. Hardwood treads with
   underlayment by on-site contractor
4. Cable rail
5. Stair 17R @ 7-9/16" each, typ.

Located above the huge double-height loft-style living-dining room space is a floating passage that connects the master bedroom to the guest bedroom.

Sobre el salón-comedor (un espacio diáfano a doble altura de estética *loft*), flota la pasarela que conecta el dormitorio principal con el de invitados.

LAKE IOSCO HOUSE
Modules: 4 Boxes

Resolution: 4 Architecture
Location: Bloomingdale, NJ, USA
Photos © RES4, Steve Hockstein | Harvard Studio

This building is a second home belonging to a single mother and young son. The house that stood formerly on the plot was dark and did not make the most of its environment. "It looked like a cave", says the owner. Together with the architects she planned this home as two linear floors that were as close as possible to the lake, offering views from every room.

Este proyecto es la segunda residencia de una madre soltera y su hijo pequeño. La casa que había antes en esta parcela era oscura y no disfrutaba del entorno. "Parecía una cueva", dice la propietaria. Junto con los arquitectos, planificaron esta residencia de dos plantas lineal tan cerca del lago como fuera posible y con vistas desde todas las habitaciones.

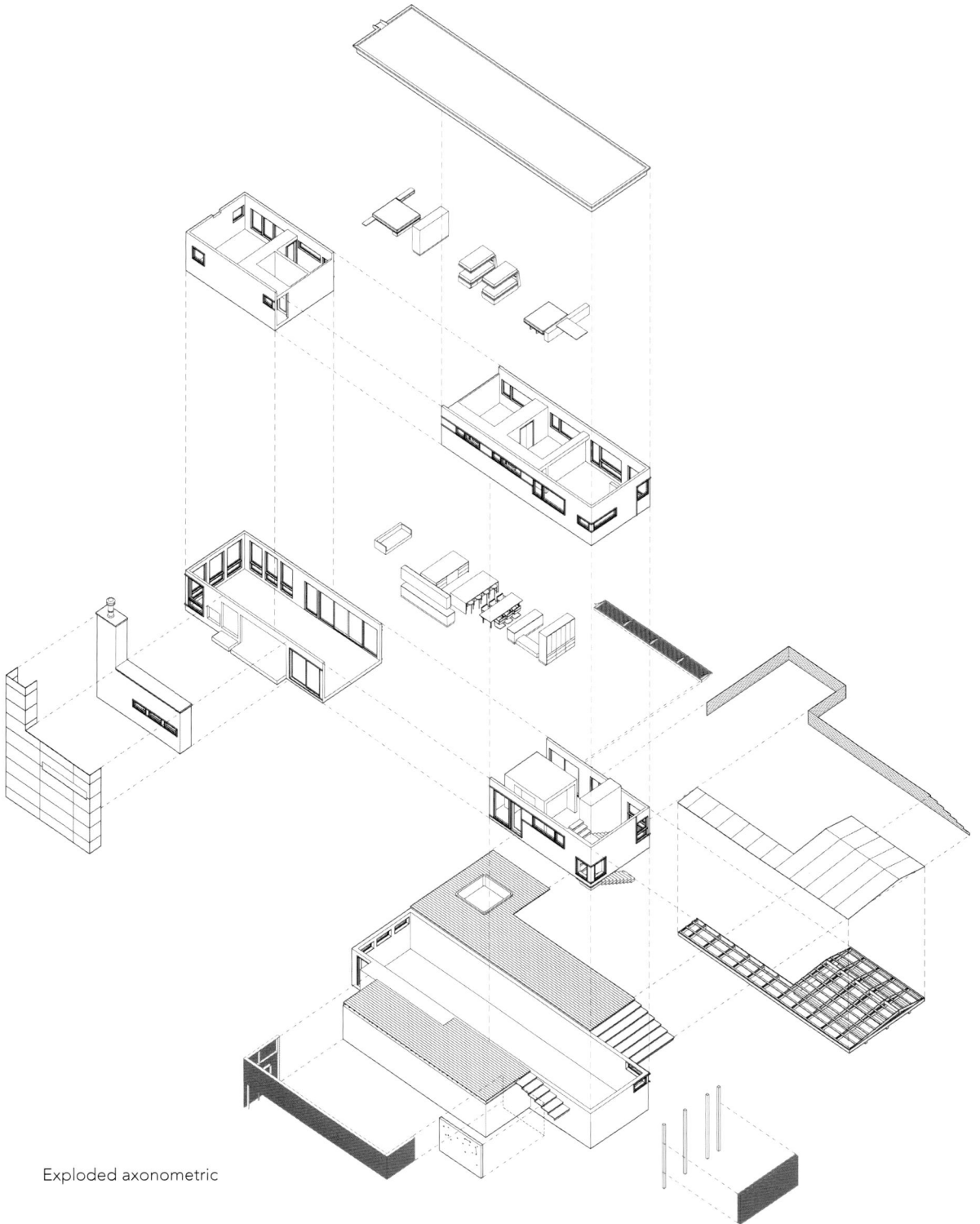

Exploded axonometric

North elevation

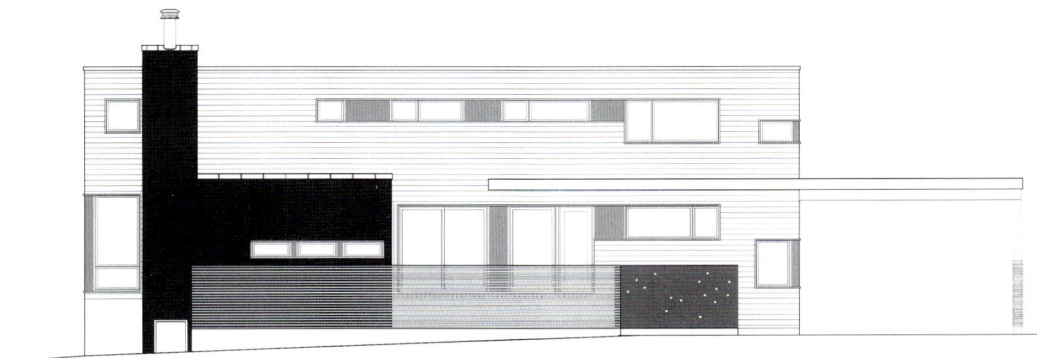

South elevation

West elevation

East elevation

The owner looked at a number of different projects that could be adjusted to meet her needs. This prefabricated four-module house met every single one.

La propietaria buscó distintos proyectos que se ajustaran a lo que quería. Esta casa prefabricada compuesta de cuatro módulos cumplía todas sus expectativas.

The large lounge, open to the dining room and kitchen, dominates the ground floor. The exterior is designed with terraces to east and west to enjoy the sunrise and sunset.

En el plano destaca el gran salón abierto al comedor y la cocina. En el diseño exterior, las terrazas al este y oeste, para contemplar el amanecer y la puesta de sol.

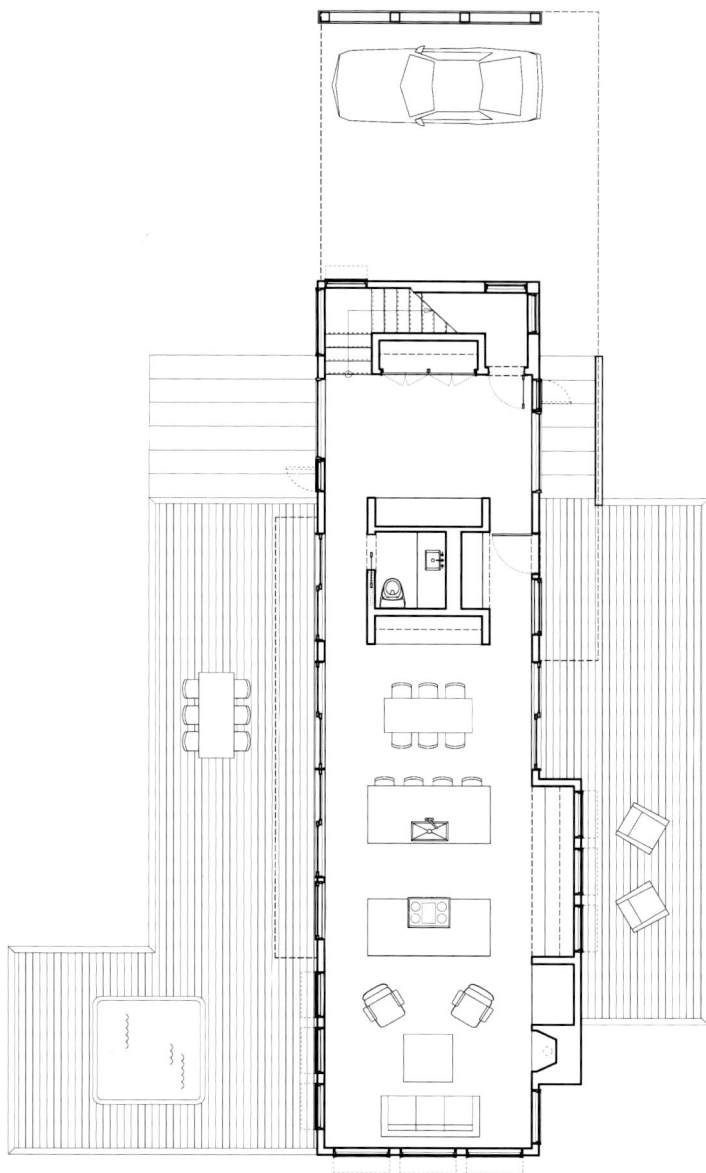

Ground floor plan

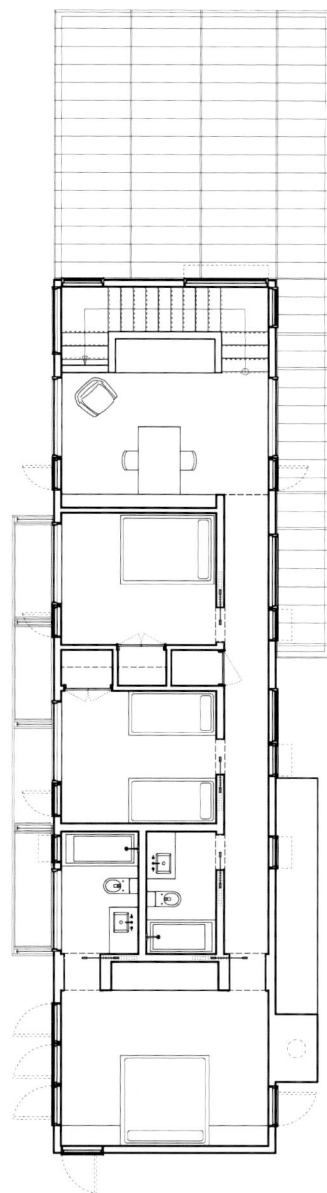

Second floor plan

On the first floor next to the stairs is an open studio, which marks the separation between the house's communal and private areas.

En la primera planta, junto a las escaleras, se encuentra un estudio abierto que marca el final del área pública y el principio de las zonas privadas.

VERMONT CABIN
Modules: 5 Boxes

Resolution: 4 architecture. Joseph Tanney, Robert Luntz
Location: Jamaica, Vermont, USA
Photos © RES4

Set alone in a clearing in the woods in the Green Mountain National Forest of Vermont, this 1614 sq ft prefab home is the place where a retired couple from Brooklyn escapes. With stunning views of nearby Stratton Mountain Ski Resort, the home is a 'Head & Tail' design, where the communal space is the 'head', and the private bar of bedrooms and baths forms the longer 'tail'. Together they form an 'L', creating an outdoor terrace to capture the western sun.

Situada en una zona aislada en el claro de un bosque, en el parque nacional Green Mountain National Forest de Vermont, esta casa prefabricada de 150 m² es el lugar donde escapa una pareja de jubilados de Brooklyn. Con vistas abrumadoras al cercano complejo de esquí Stratton Mountain, la vivienda es un diseño de "cara o cruz", donde la zona común es la "cara" y la sección privada que contiene los dormitorios y los baños es la "cruz". Unidas forman una "L", creando una terraza descubierta para captar el sol del oeste.

10

9

8

7

6

2

1

3

5

4

1. Entry
2. Laundry
3. Kitchen
4. Dining room
5. Living room
6. Media room
7. Bathroom
8. Bedroom
9. Master bathroom
10. Master bedroom

Floor plan

The exterior is clad in a maintenance-free corrugated Cor-ten metal panel system to withstand the harsh Vermont winters. Accents of cedar siding tie the strategically placed windows together.

El exterior está revestido con un sistema de paneles de acero corten corrugado que no necesita mantenimiento, para resistir los duros inviernos de Vermont. El revestimiento de cedro, dispuesto de manera estratégica, une a las ventanas.

The home is powered by a 3,000 KwH solar array with a back-up generator and below grade propane tank just in case the sun is non-existent for an extended period of time.

La casa se alimenta con paneles solares de 3000 kWh con un generador suplementario y un tanque de propano de bajo grado por si no hubiera sol durante un largo periodo de tiempo.

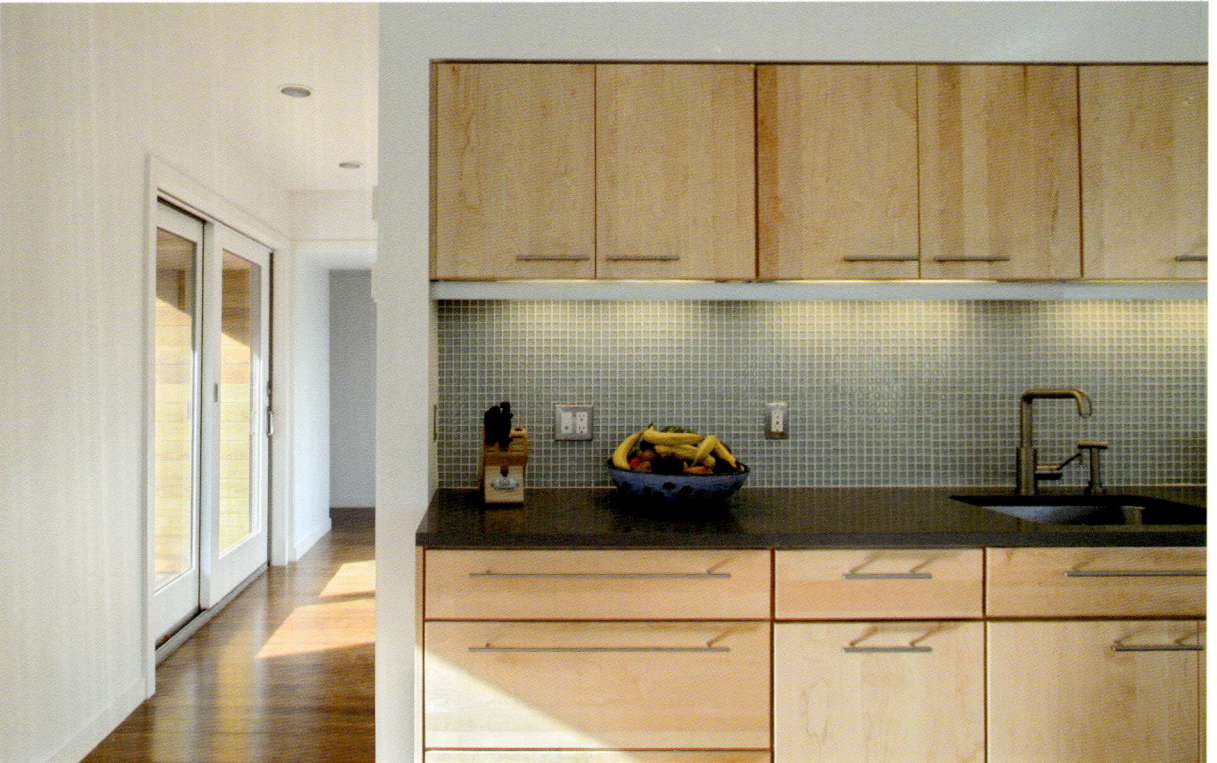

DWELL HOME

Modules: 5 Boxes

Resolution: 4 architecture. Joseph Tanney, Robert Luntz
Location: Pittsboro, NC, USA
Photos © Jerry Markatos, Roger Davies

The Dwell Home is situated on a hilly site among 7 wooded acres. The home takes full advantage of it's natural surroundings: bringing in the woodland views and natural light through plentiful windows, generously sized decks off the front and rear facades, and a roof deck with an outdoor fireplace. With about 2368 sq ft divided among five prefabricated modules, the home offers compact and efficient quarters made up of large open living spaces and cosy private enclaves.

La Dwell Home está ubicada en un terreno montañoso entre casi tres hectáreas de arboleda. La casa saca partido de su entorno natural, ofreciendo vistas al bosque y luz natural a través de una gran cantidad de ventanas, terrazas de un generoso tamaño en la fachada principal y en la trasera, y una azotea con una chimenea descubierta. Con un total de casi 220 m² divididos en cinco módulos prefabricados, la vivienda ofrece habitaciones compactas y eficientes creadas a partir de grandes espacios abiertos y acogedores enclaves privados.

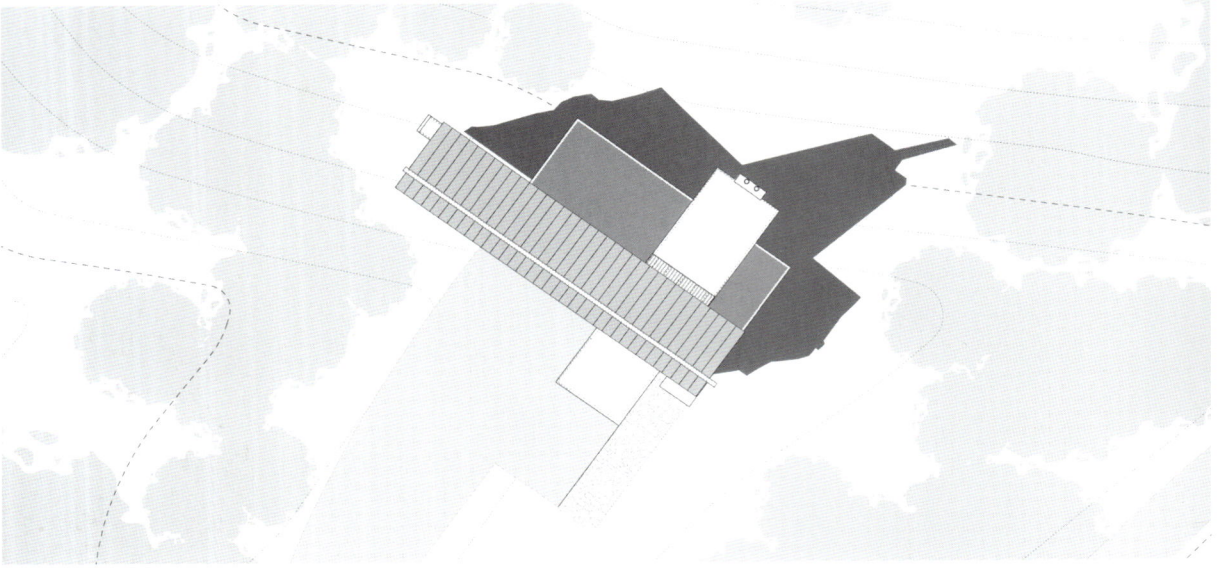

Site plan

PREFABRICATED CONSTRUCTION
1. Communal module
2. Private module
3. Stair module
4. Storage module
5. Roof module

SITE WORK
A. Kitchen saddlebag
B. Living room fireplace / chimney
C. Balcony
D. Patio
E. Cedar siding
F. Brise soleil

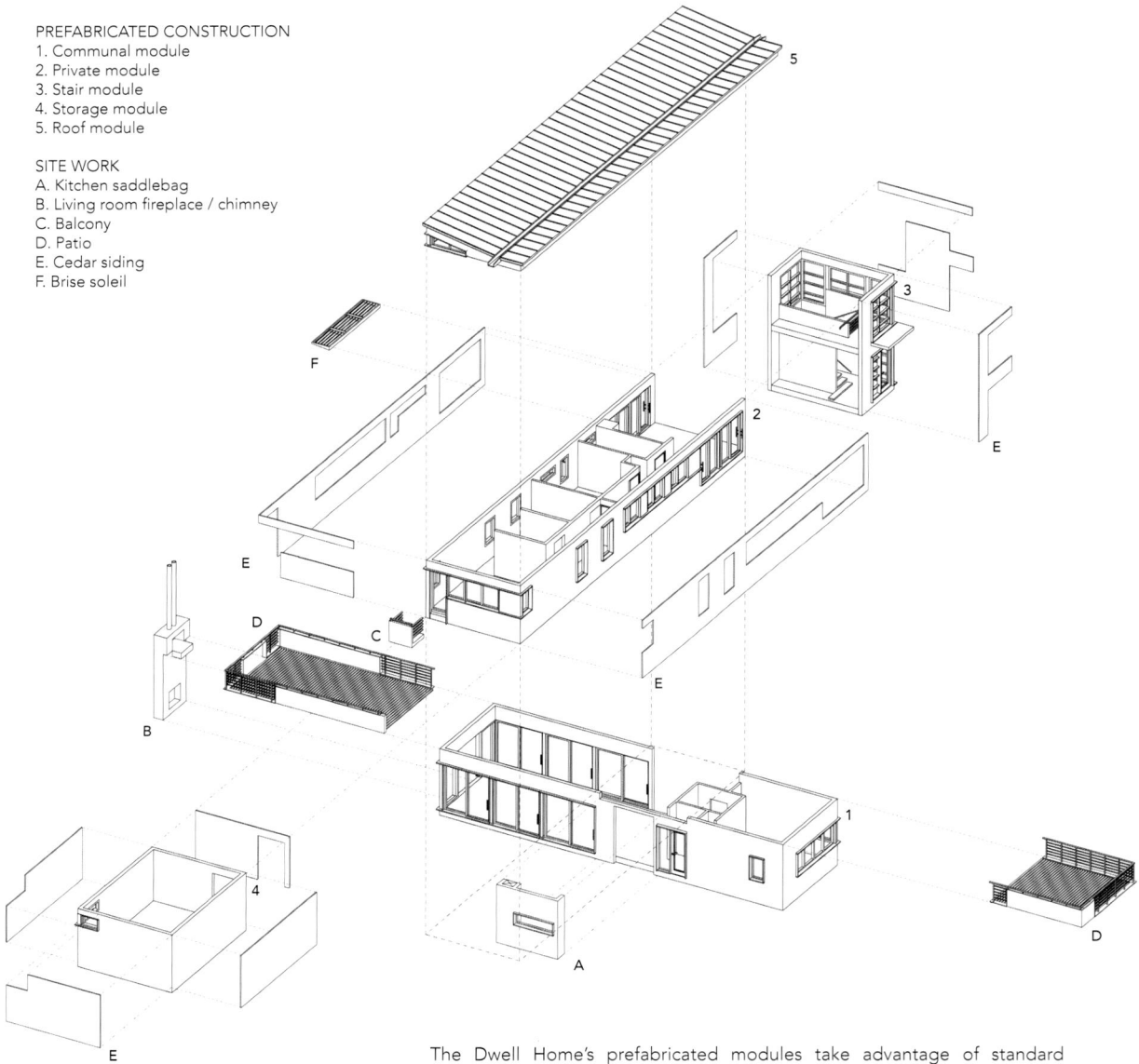

Axonometry

The Dwell Home's prefabricated modules take advantage of standard modular methods of construction and can be inexpensively produced in a factory environment. The modules are trucked to site and craned onto a site-built concrete foundation which houses all mechanical systems. The house is finished with additional site construction of elements that are not practical or economical to produce using off-site construction.

Se utilizó el método de construcción modular estándar para los módulos prefabricados de la Dwell Home, ya que pueden producirse económicamente en una fábrica. Los módulos se transportaron al lugar en un camión y se colocaron mediante una grúa sobre una base de hormigón construida en el emplazamiento, que disponía de todos los sistemas mecánicos. La vivienda se terminó con elementos de construcción adicionales que no son prácticos o económicos de producir en fábrica.

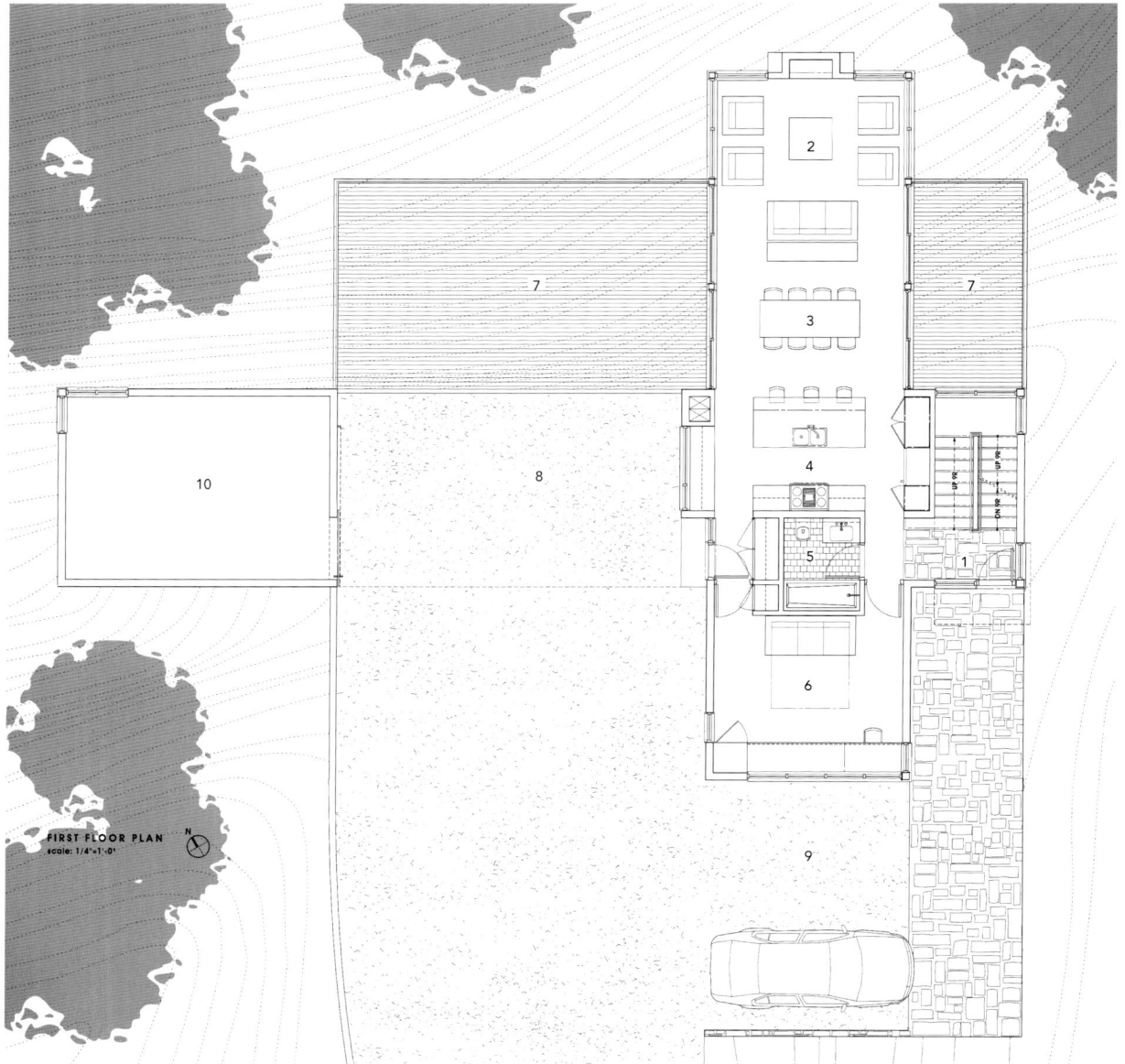

FIRST FLOOR PLAN
scale: 1/4"=1'-0"

First floor

1. Main entrance
2. Living
3. Dining
4. Kitchen
5. Bathroom
6. Office / bedroom
7. Deck
8. Covered packing
9. Parking
10. Storage

1. Office
2. Bathroom
3. Bedroom
4. Master bath
5. Closet / dressing
6. Master bedroom
7. Terrace
8. Balcony

Second floor

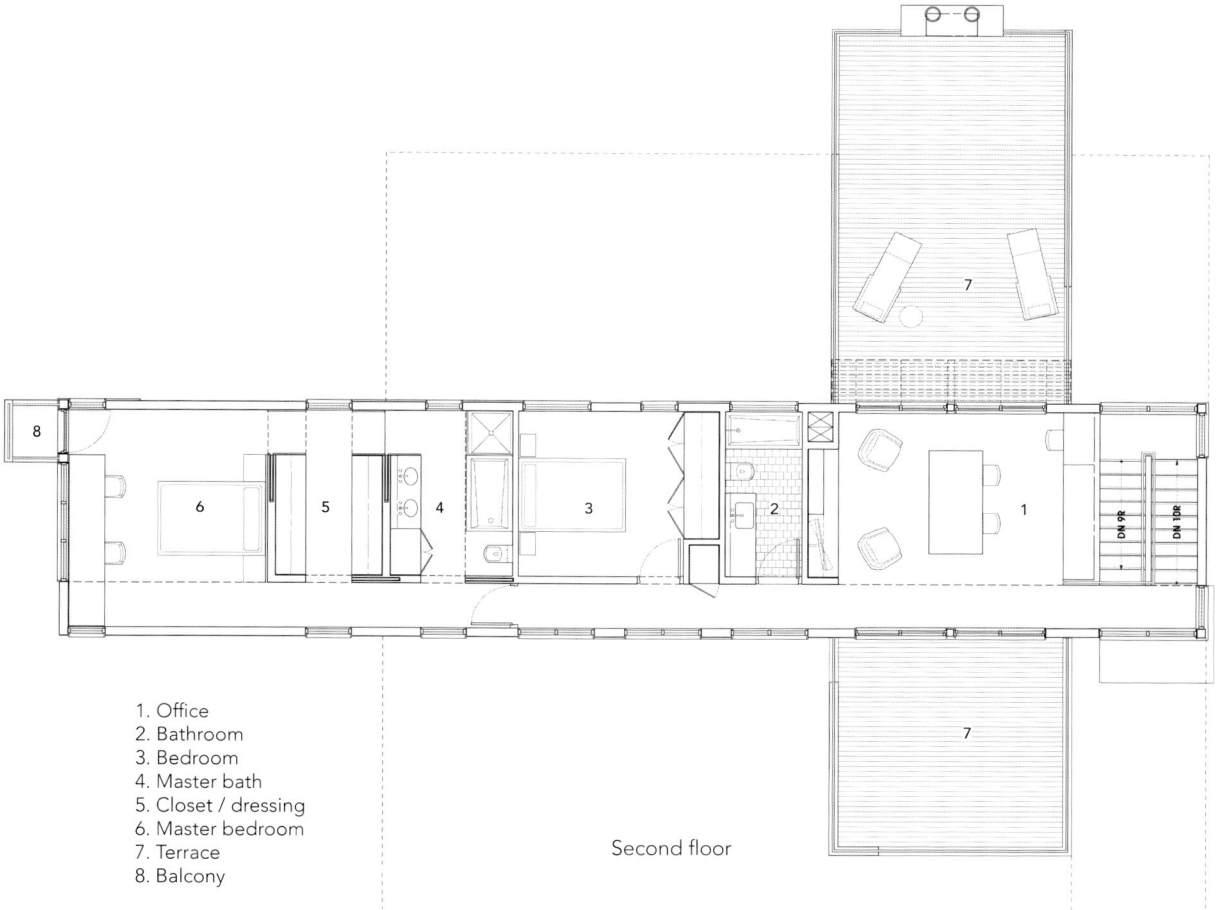

To meet the necessity of creating a liveable floor plan and a well-orchestrated flow of space, the ground floor is an open plan module containing a living room, dining area, and a kitchen that can be entirely open to the outside or enclosed by a curtain.

Para cumplir con la necesidad de crear una planta habitable y una fluidez del espacio bien organizada, la planta baja es un módulo espacioso que contiene la sala de estar, el comedor y una cocina que puede ser totalmente exterior o separarse con una cortina.

Sensitive to the clients' desire for more defined communal/private spaces, the private spaces are more compartmentalized making up the second story volume of the home.

Conscientes de que el cliente deseaba unos espacios comunes y privados más definidos, las zonas privadas están más compartimentadas al construir un volumen en el segundo piso de la casa.

NORTICOTE
Modules: 5 Boxes

Modscape
Location: Northcote, VIC, Australia
Photos © Chris Daile

The highlight here is the simplicity of the house as seen from the street, which belies its real depth. Composed of five prefabricated modules placed on two off-centred planes, this home redefines the concept of modern family living. It invites us to use our imagination and embrace passive design when creating our home.

En este proyecto destaca la sobriedad de la casa vista desde la calle, que no hace sospechar la profundidad del plano. Compuesta por cinco módulos prefabricados ubicados en dos plantas desfasadas, esta residencia redefine el concepto de hogar moderno para una familia y nos invita a usar la imaginación y el diseño pasivo a la hora de idear nuestra vivienda.

Building perspective

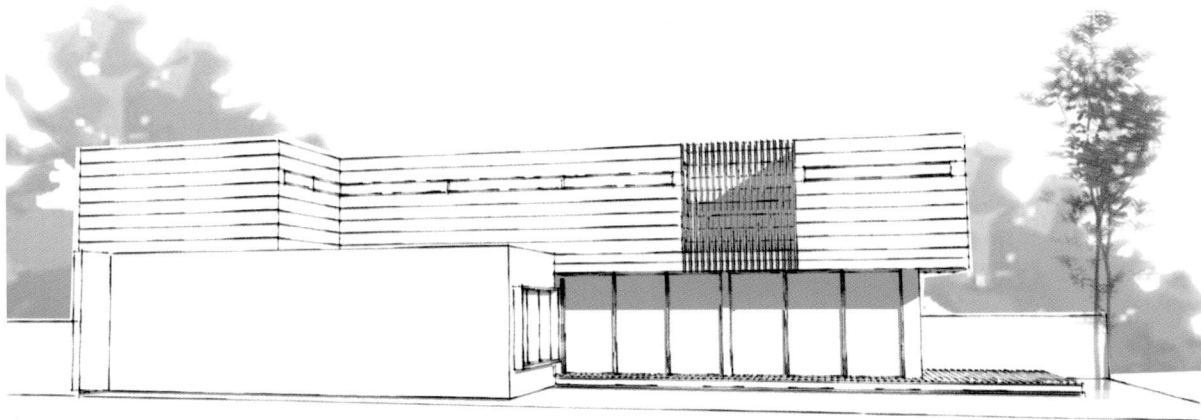

Building perspectives

Closed to the street, the front façade is also the garage. This floor also includes an open-plan space comprising kitchen, dining room and lounge, open to a terrace.

La fachada a la calle, cerrada, también es el garaje. En esta planta también hay un amplio espacio, abierto a una terraza, que engloba cocina, comedor y salón.

The windows and glass doors open to the back garden, giving continuity between inside and out while maintaining privacy for the family.

Los ventanales y puertas de cristal se abren al jardín posterior, para dar continuidad del espacio interior al exterior y preservar la intimidad de la familia.

6.14 m

J

K   L

P   M   Q

N

O   L

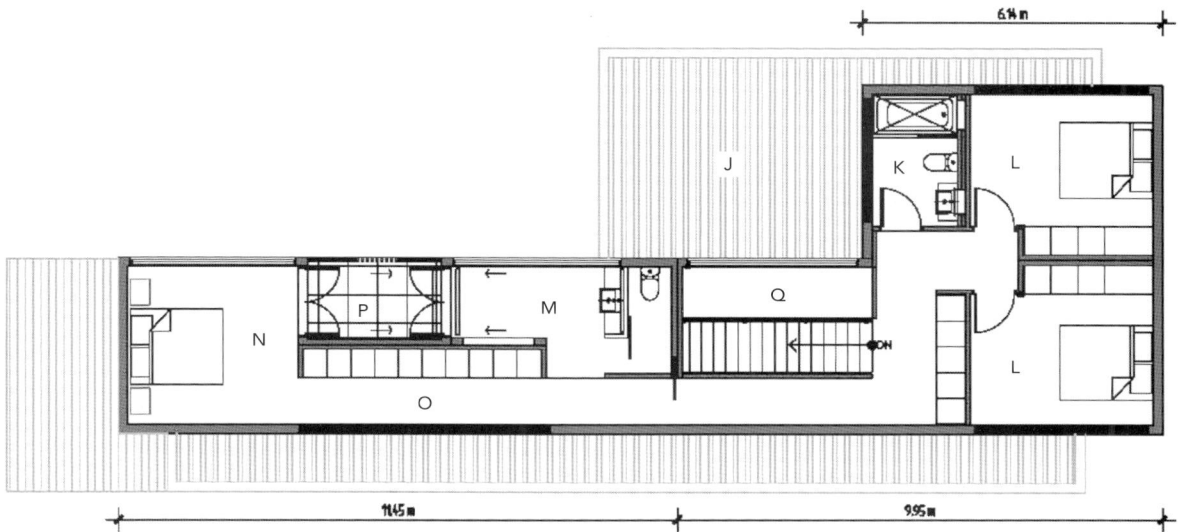

Second floor plan

11.15 m   9.95 m

A. Entry
B. Garage
C. Study
D. Toilet
E. Laundry room
F. Living area
G. Kitchen
H. Dining area
I. Deck
J. Roof below
K. Bathroom
L. Bedroom
M. Ensuite
N. Master bedroom
O. Walk-in-closet
P. Balcony
Q. Void

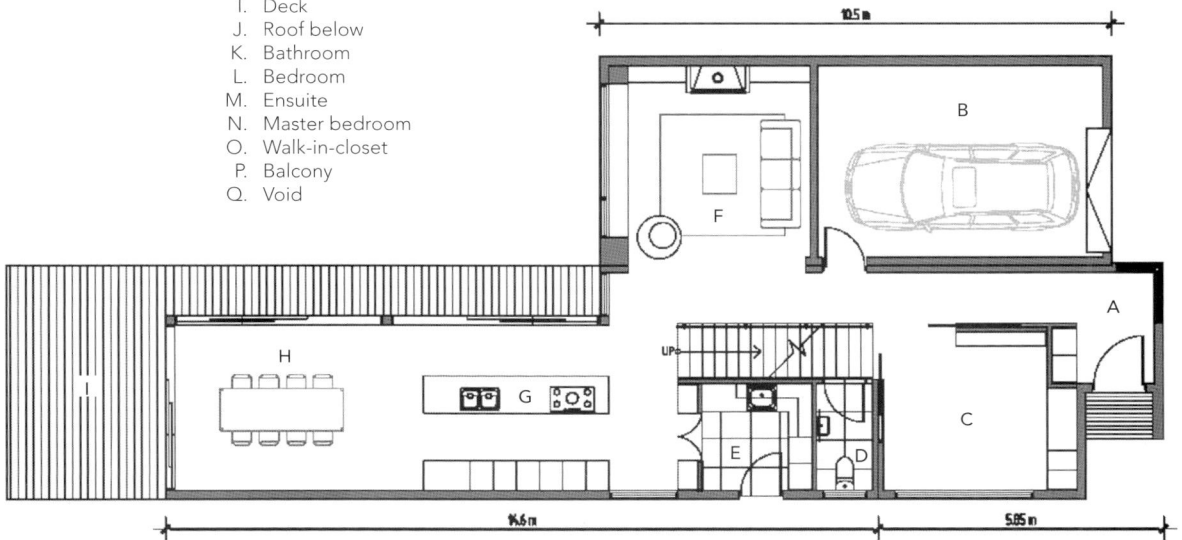

10.5 m

B

F

A

UP→

H

G   C

I   E   D

Ground floor plan

14.6 m   5.85 m

X-LINE 014
Modules: 6 Boxes

Hive Modular
Location: Calgary, AB, Canada
Photos © Hive Modular

Maximum space and light. The owners wanted a new house that would not contradict the existing aesthetic of the neighbourhood and this prefabricated six-module home meets all their requirements. The heart of the home is the living room with fireplace. The double-height ceiling and large windows within the front and back façades bring a feeling of light and space to the home.

Más espacio y luz. Los propietarios querían una nueva casa que no chocase frontalmente con la estética del vecindario. Esta vivienda prefabricada compuesta de seis módulos cumple con todos los requisitos. El corazón del proyecto es el salón con chimenea. Su doble altura y los amplios ventanales a la fachada principal y trasera llenan de luz y espacio todo el hogar.

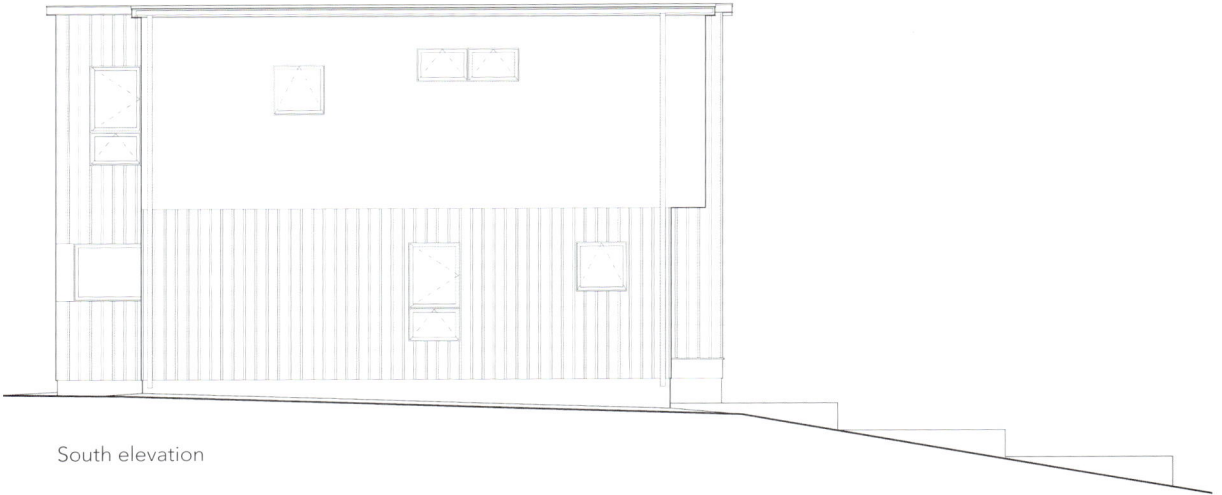

South elevation

West elevation

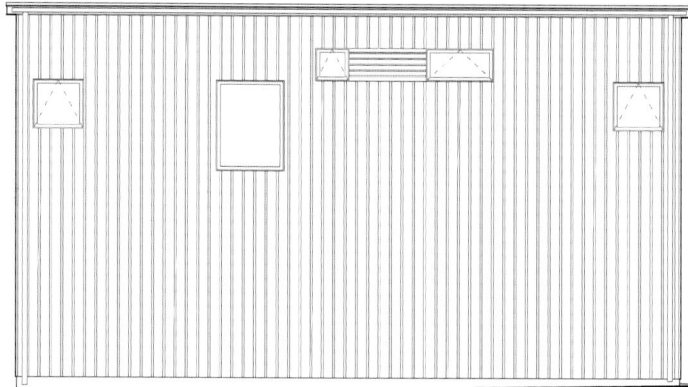

North elevation

East elevation

The units were built entirely at the Hive Modular factory. They were then moved to their final location to be installed and assembled in situ.

Los módulos se construyeron íntegramente en la fábrica de Hive Modular. Posteriormente se trasladaron a su ubicación final para el montaje y ensamblaje in situ.

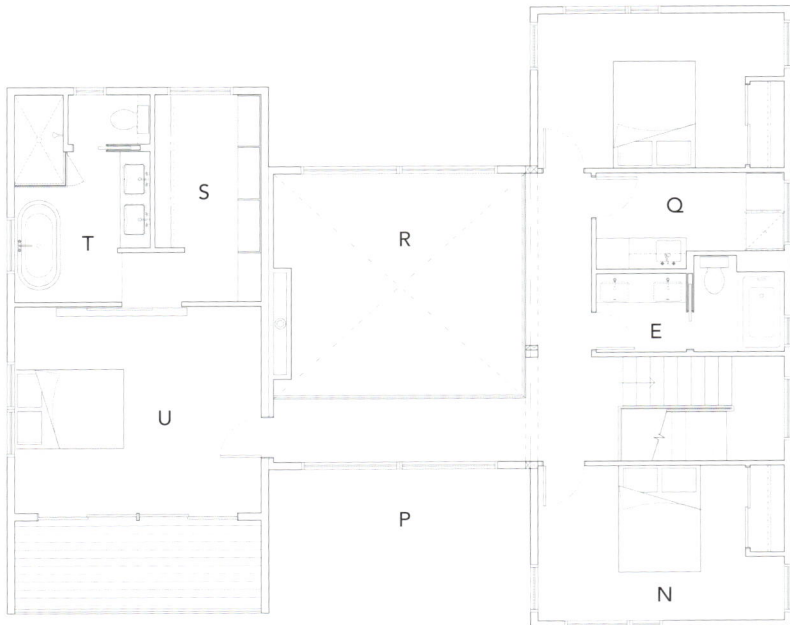

Upper floor plan

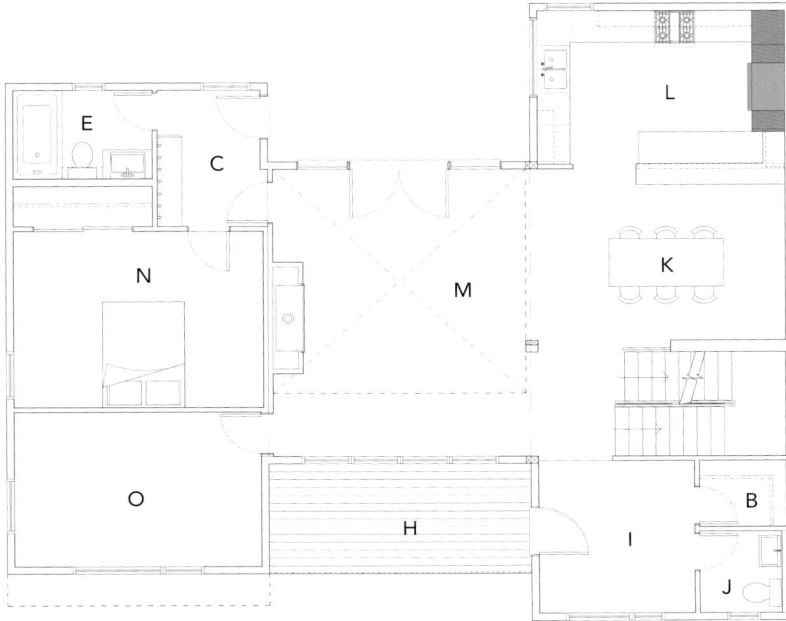

Main floor plan

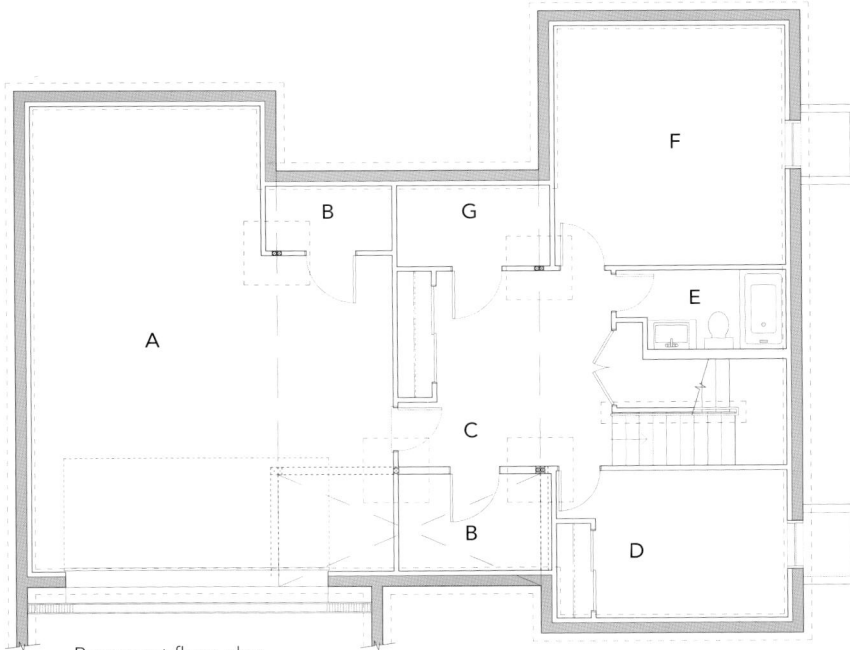

Basement floor plan

A. Garage
B. Storage
C. Mud room
D. Craft room
E. Bathroom
F. Theater
G. Mechanical room
H. Entry porch
I. Entry foyer
J. Powder room
K. Dining room
L. Kitchen
M. Living room
N. Bedroom
O. Den
P. Hallway
Q. Laundry room
R. Open to below
S. Walk-in-closet
T. Master bathroom
U. Master bedroom

Plenty of sunlight yet plenty of privacy. The house features large windows and a terrace on the front facade, away from the street and neighbours.

Mucha luz solar, preservando la intimidad de los ocupantes. La casa ofrece grandes ventanales y una terraza en la fachada delantera, lejos de los vecinos y de la calle.

Downstairs is a spacious open-plan area comprising living room, dining room and kitchen. The large windows enable light to flow throughout the property.

En la planta baja se abre una amplia zona diáfana que comprende el salón, el comedor y la cocina. Sus grandes ventanales hacen que fluya la luz a toda la residencia.

HOUSE ON SUNSET RIDGE
Modules: 6 Boxes

Resolution: 4 Architecture. Joseph Tanney, Robert Luntz
Location: Norfolk, CT, USA
Photos © RES4, Paul Warchol

Conceived as a weekend sanctuary for a New York family, this home enjoys a privileged location on a hill offering magnificent views. It consists of six exemplary eco-friendly modules (with green roof, wood from managed forests and an energy-efficient boiler...) with terraces, windows and a conservatory to provide maximum natural light.

Concebida como un santuario de fin de semana para una familia neoyorquina, goza de una ubicación privilegiada, sobre una colina con magníficas vistas. Consta de seis módulos ejemplarmente ecosostenibles (cubierta ajardinada, madera de bosques controlados, caldera de alta eficiencia energética…) y sus terrazas, ventanales y porche acristalado le permiten maximizar la luz solar.

110

This spectacular outdoor fireplace creates a year-round multipurpose entertainment space, even in the cold climate of Connecticut.

Esta espectacular chimenea al aire libre habilita la terraza como un espacio de ocio multiusos durante todo el año, incluso en el clima frío de Connecticut.

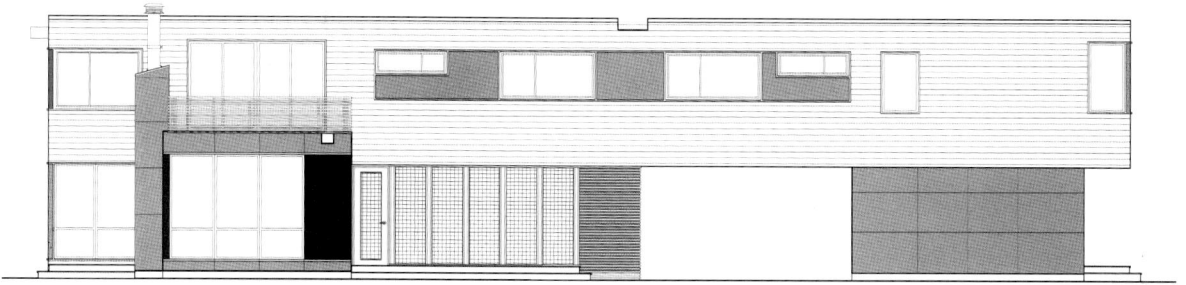

North elevation

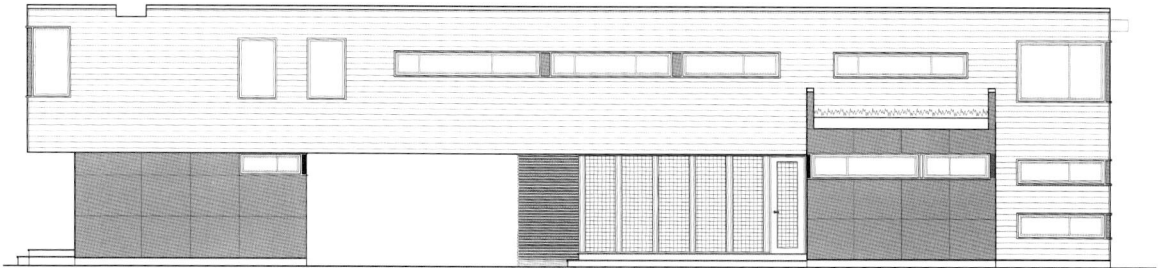

South elevation

West elevation

East elevation

0 2 6 9 12 FT

112

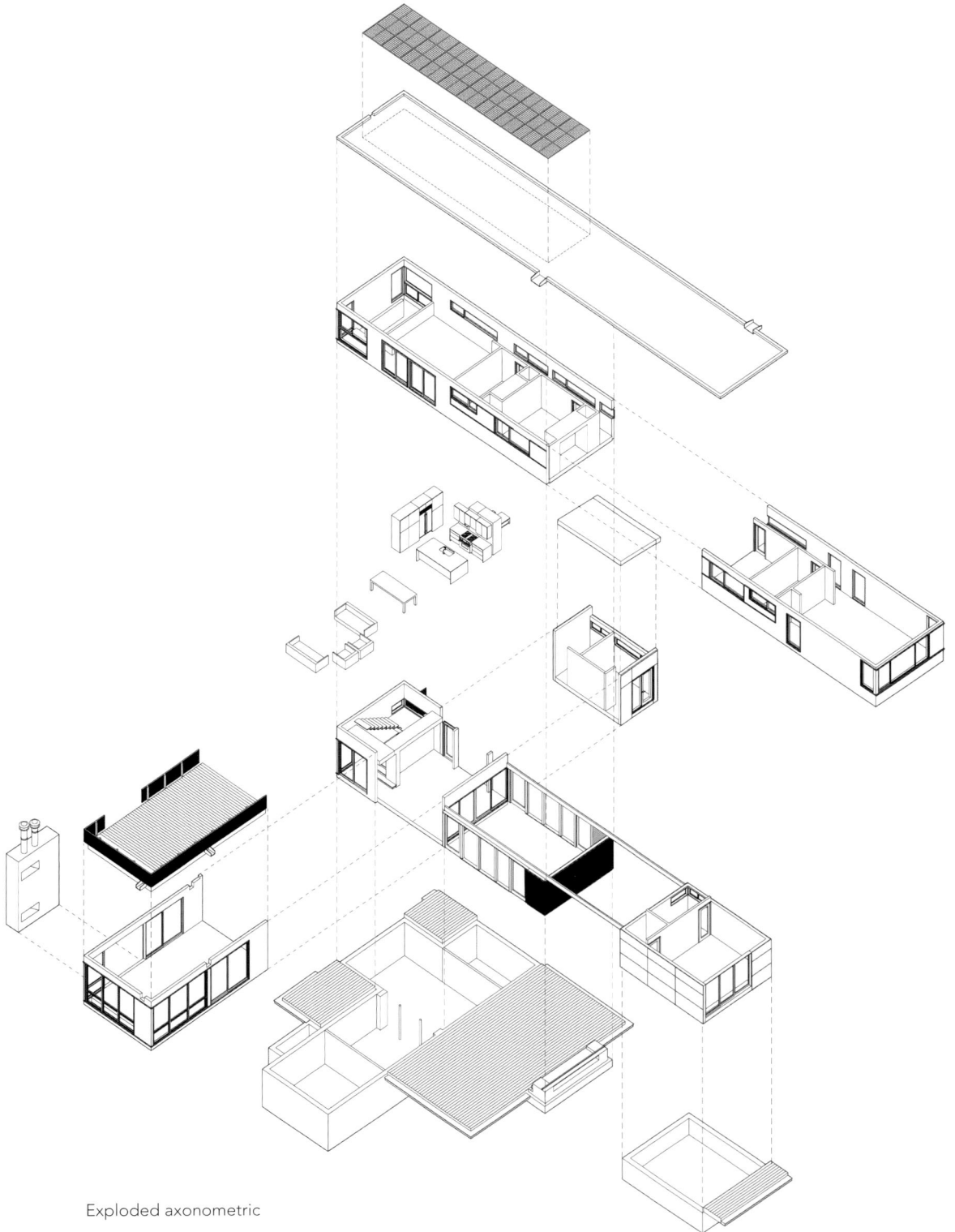

Exploded axonometric

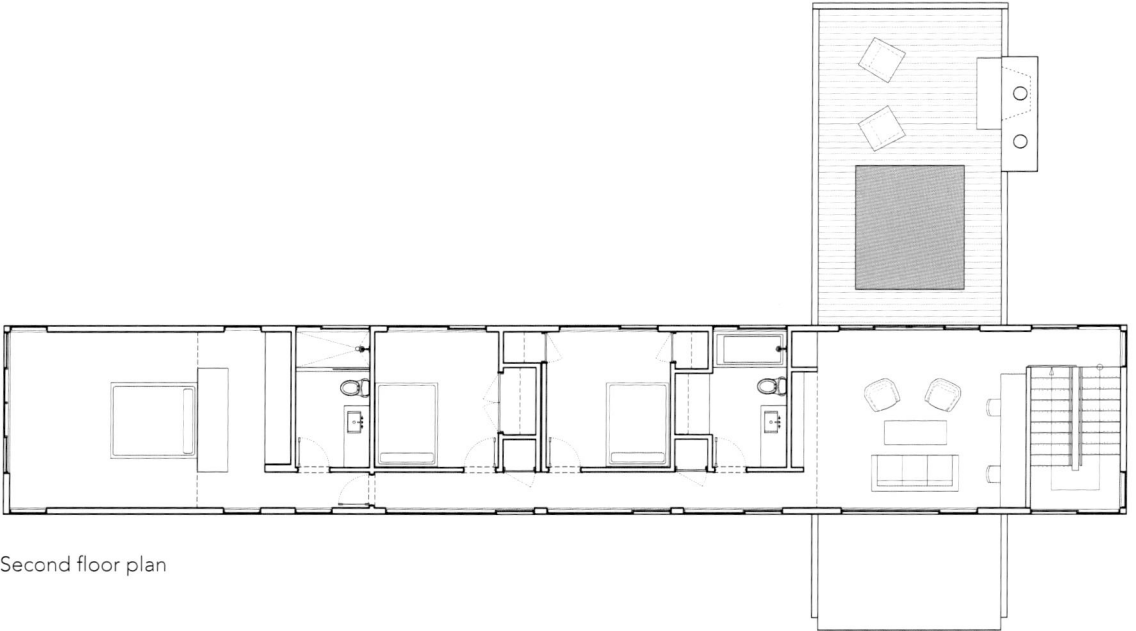

Second floor plan

The common rooms (dining room, kitchen…) are on the ground floor while the upper floor, which houses the bedrooms and bathrooms, is more private.

La planta baja contiene las estancias comunes (comedor, cocina…). La superior tiene un carácter más privado, ya que alberga los baños y dormitorios.

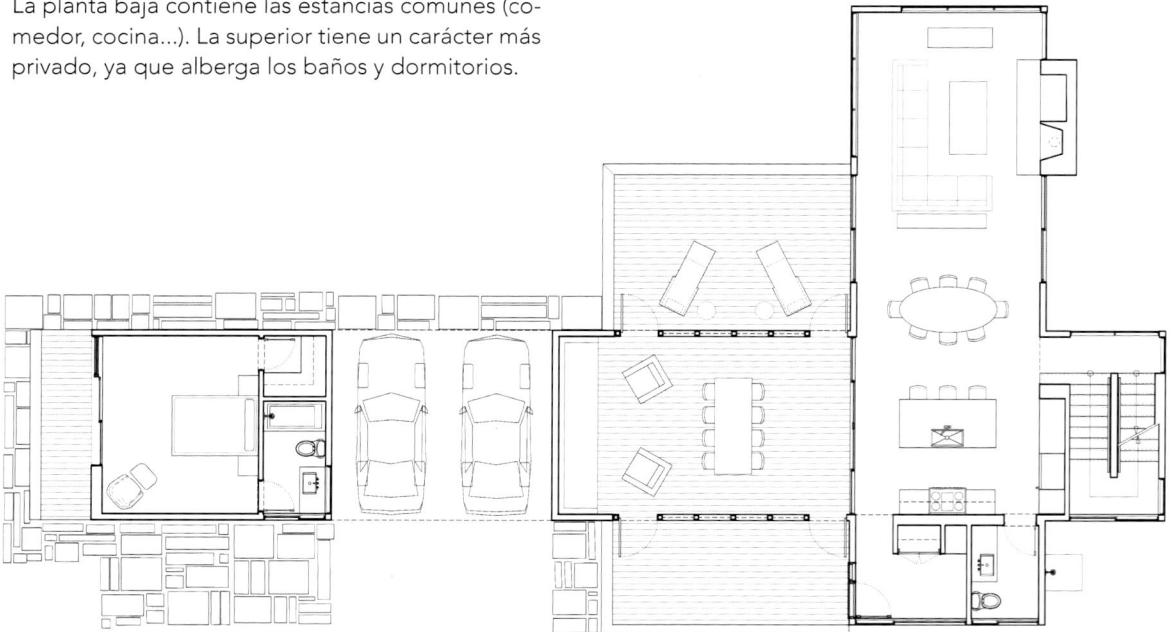

Ground floor plan

BERKSHIRE HOUSE

Modules: 6 Boxes

Resolution: 4 Architecture. Joseph Tanney, Robert Luntz
Location: Palenville, NY, USA
Photos © RES4

Berkshire House is a modification of the 2-Bar Bridge, L Series typology; the Berkshire House is a further development of the original concept for the Dwell Home, the first fully designed prototype of an economical prefabricated Modern Modular home, designed by Resolution: 4 Architecture. Each RES4 Prefab design is modified and engineered specifically for each client and site.

La Berkshire House es una modificación del 2-Bar Bridge, que pertenece a la tipología de serie L. Esta vivienda es una evolución del concepto original de la Dwell Home, el primer prototipo completamente diseñado de una casa Modern Modular prefabricada económicamente y creada por Resolution: 4 Architecture. Cada diseño de la RES4 Prefab se modifica y produce específicamente para cada cliente y lugar.

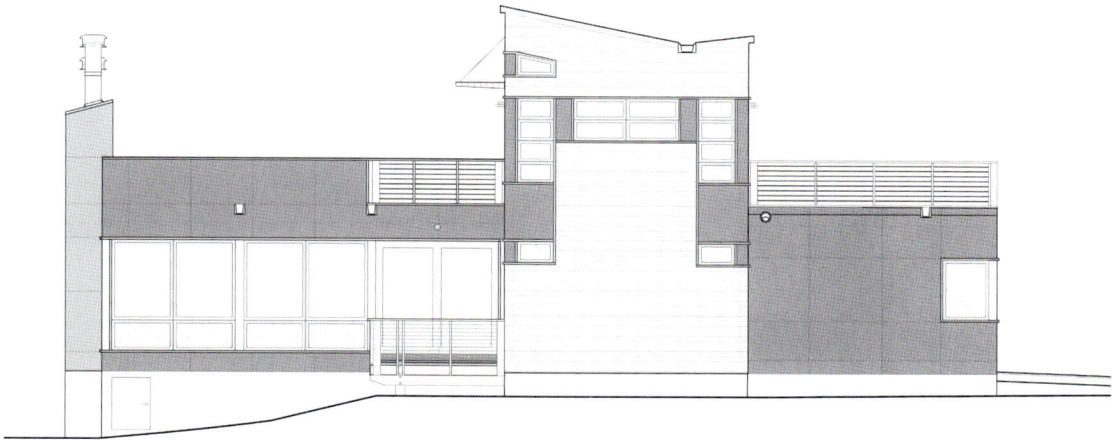

East elevation

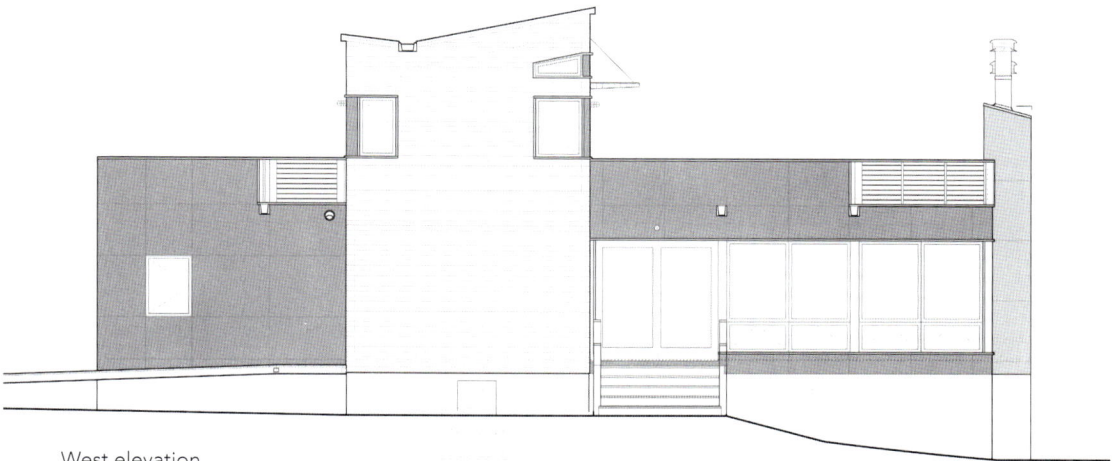

West elevation

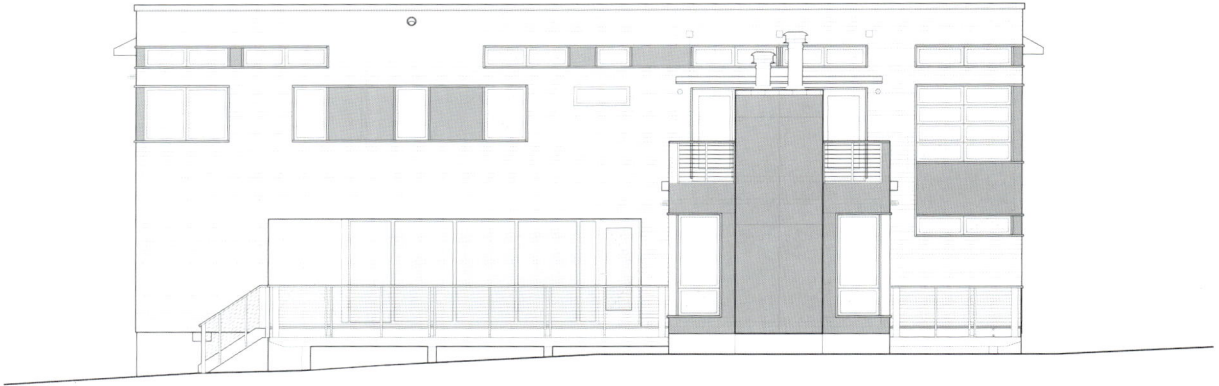

North elevation

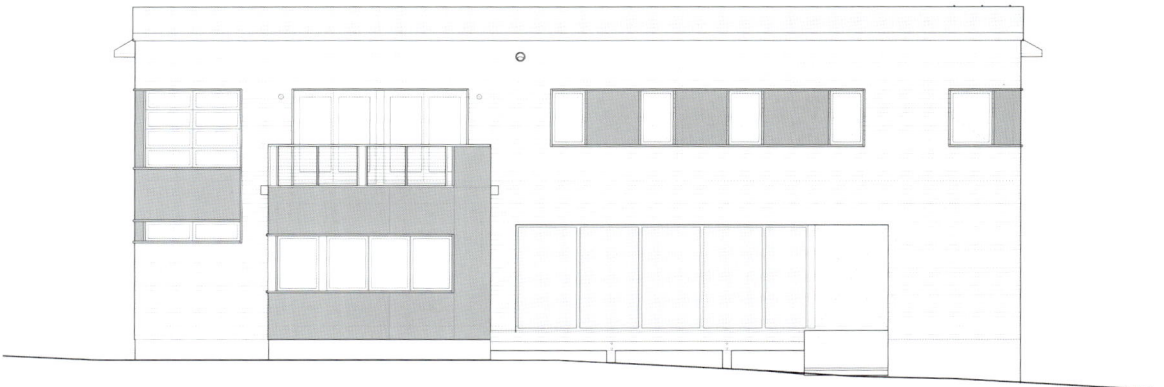

South elevation

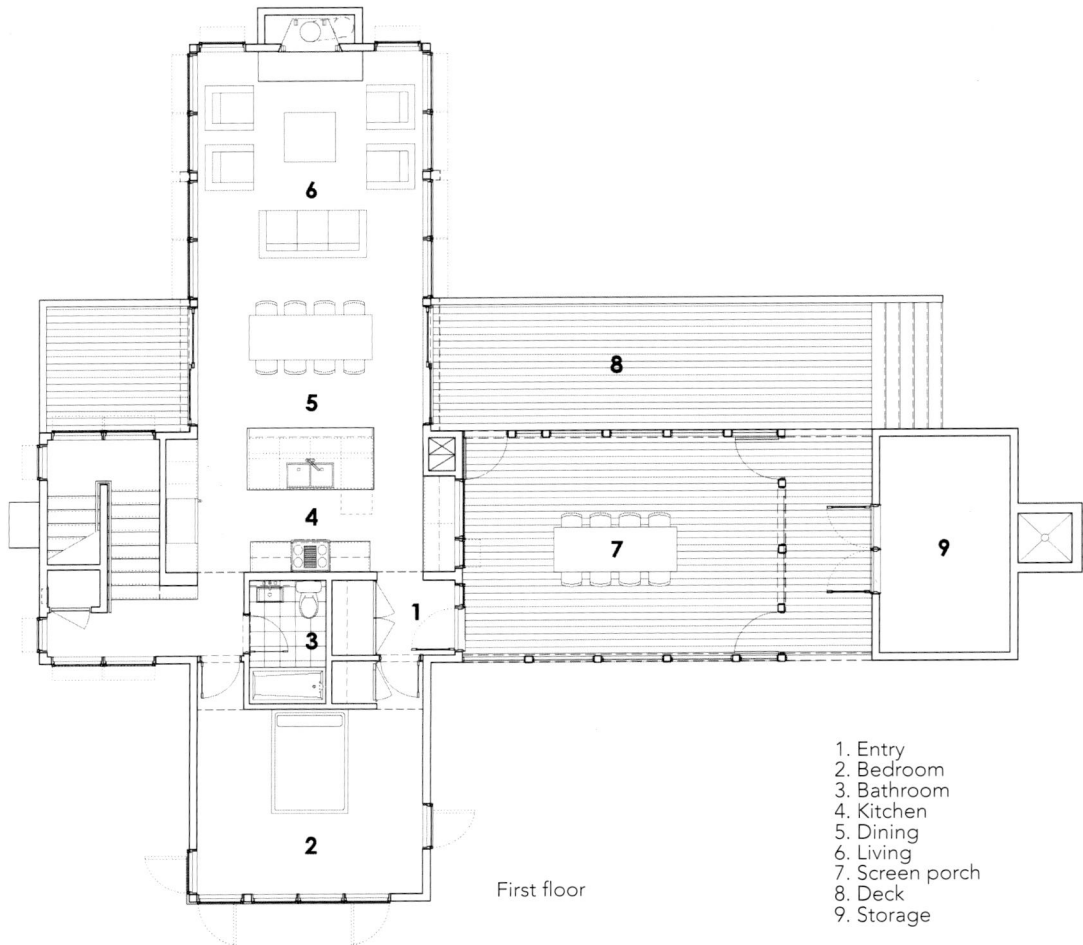

First floor

1. Entry
2. Bedroom
3. Bathroom
4. Kitchen
5. Dining
6. Living
7. Screen porch
8. Deck
9. Storage

Green roofs have also been introduced into many RES4 Prefab. These roofs significantly decrease the amount of storm-water run-off, building energy requirements, air and noise pollution, provide for useable outdoor patio spaces, and give way to a longer lasting roof system.

También se han introducido tejados ecológicos en las casas de RES4: disminuyen significativamente la escorrentía del agua de lluvia, los requerimientos energéticos de la casa y la contaminación atmosférica y acústica; proporcionan espacios exteriores utilizables y dan paso a un sistema de tejado más duradero.

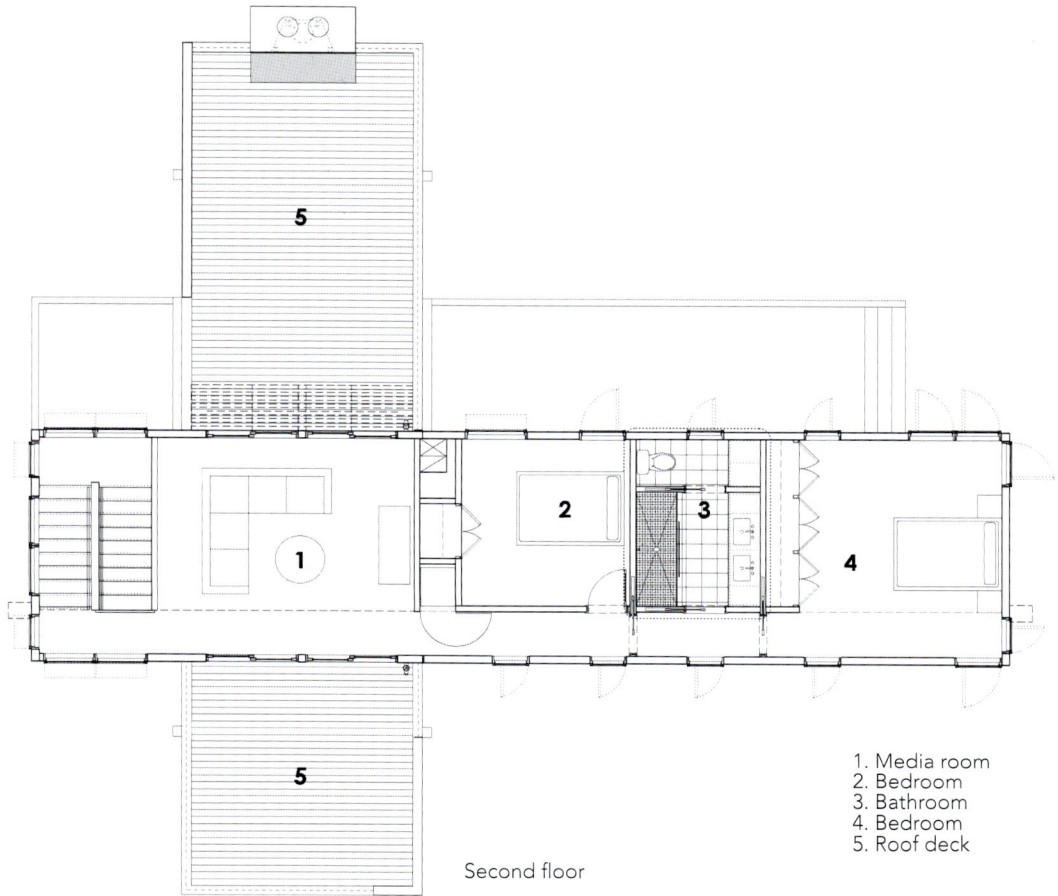

1. Media room
2. Bedroom
3. Bathroom
4. Bedroom
5. Roof deck

Second floor

SWINGLINE
Modules: 7 Boxes

Resolution: 4 Architecture. Joseph Tanney, Robert Luntz
Location: Wainscott, NY, USA
Photos © RES4, Miko Almaleh

Located on a wooded three-acre site in South Hampton, New York, The Swingline aka Zim-Wex is a 4542 sq ft year-round playhouse house for two women and their four kids who split time between their New York City brownstone and the Hamptons. With numerous bedrooms, a guest room, a media room with floor to ceiling windows, screened porches, decks, a pool house, amongst other amenities, the house was built to entertain and indulge its inhabitants.

Ubicada en una arboleda de casi 1,3 hectáreas en South Hampton, Nueva York, la Swingline, también conocida como Zim-Wex, es una casa de 422 m² destinada a la diversión durante todo el año para dos mujeres y sus cuatro hijos, que dividen su tiempo entre su casa de piedra rojiza de Nueva York y la de South Hampton. Con muchos dormitorios, una habitación de invitados, una sala para ver la televisión con ventanales que van del suelo al techo, porches apantallados, terrazas, una piscina cubierta, entre otras comodidades, la casa se diseñó para entretener y satisfacer a sus habitantes.

Long elevations

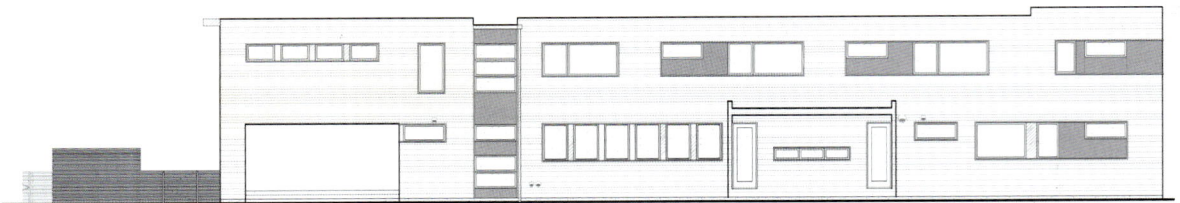

The 34m. long façade is covered in a singular texture of clear cedar intermitted by cement board and window punches.

La fachada de 34 metros de largo está cubierta por una singular textura de cedro puro intermitida por un tablero de cemento y perforaciones para las ventanas.

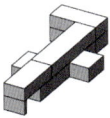

Swingline typology

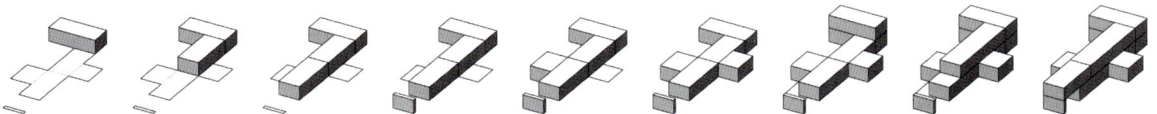

Modules of implementation: set process

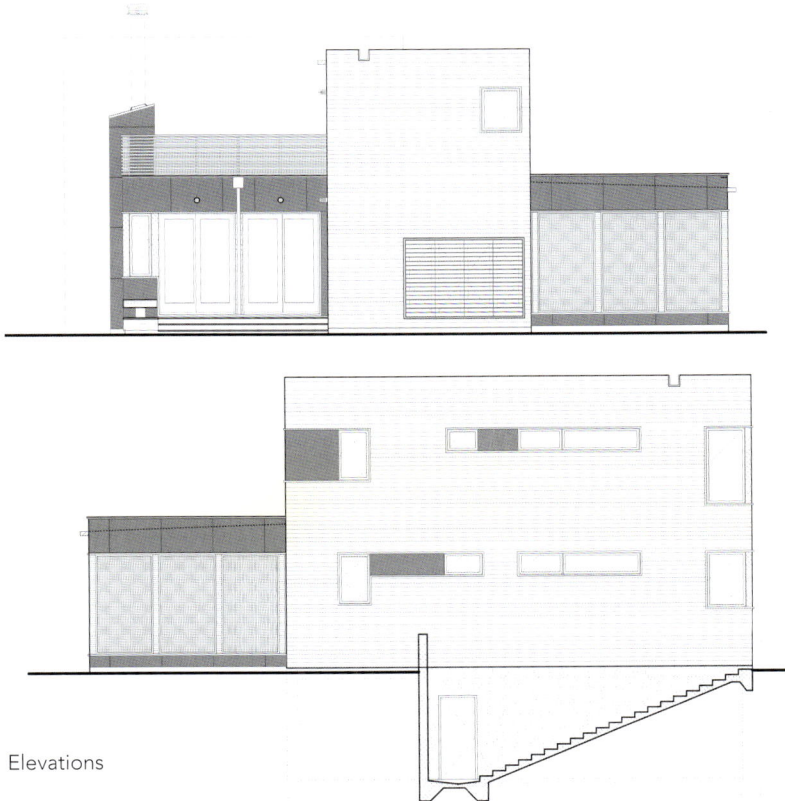

Elevations

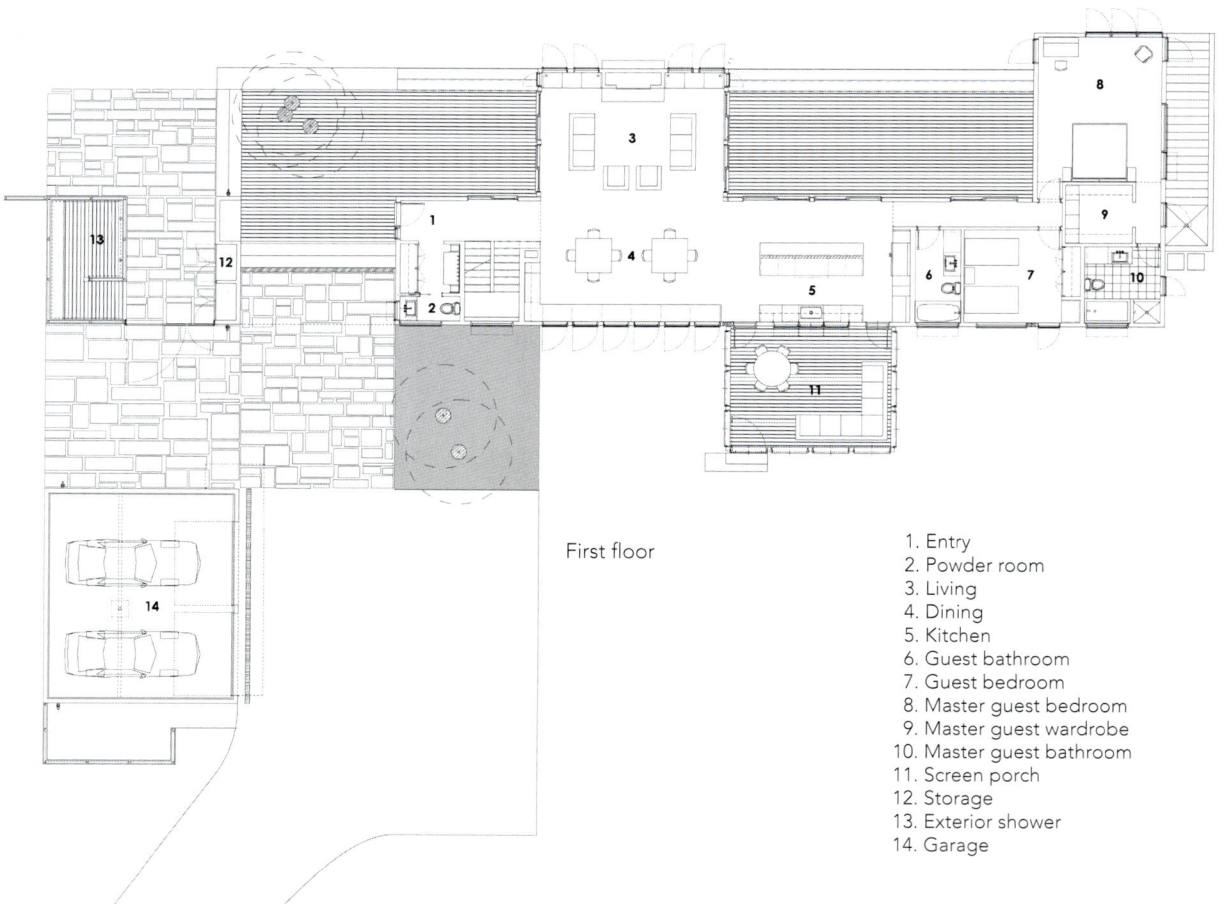

First floor

1. Entry
2. Powder room
3. Living
4. Dining
5. Kitchen
6. Guest bathroom
7. Guest bedroom
8. Master guest bedroom
9. Master guest wardrobe
10. Master guest bathroom
11. Screen porch
12. Storage
13. Exterior shower
14. Garage

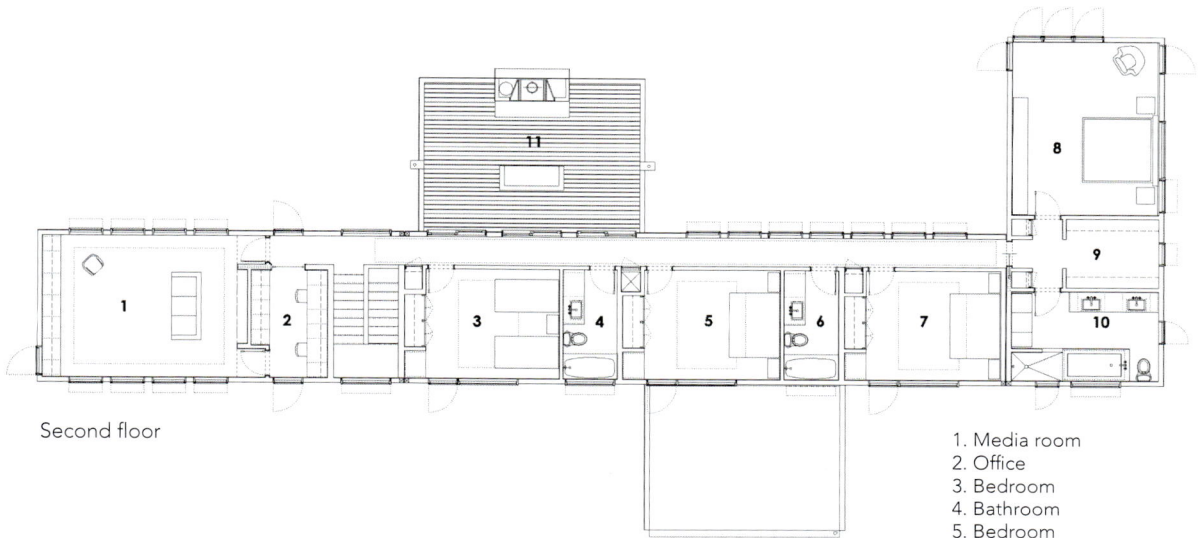

Second floor

1. Media room
2. Office
3. Bedroom
4. Bathroom
5. Bedroom
6. Bathroom
7. Bedroom
8. Master bedroom
9. Master wardrobe
10. Master bathroom
11. Roof deck

TREEHOUSE CABO DA ROCA

Modules: 11 Boxes

Appleton e Domingos Arquitectos
Location: Cabo da Roca, Azóia, Portugal
Photos © Fernando Guerra, FG+SG and Pedro Ferreira

Situated in a coastal area near Lisbon, this 2,691 sq ft house consists of two off-centred storeys, creating a less compact space as well as more defined outside areas (patios and terraces) which connect the house to its external surroundings. The building is constructed entirely in wood and the assembly of the 11 modules took just 12 hours.

Esta casa de 250 m² situada en una zona costera cercana a Lisboa presenta dos plantas desfasadas, que permiten un volumen menos compacto y la creación de espacios exteriores más definidos (patios y terrazas), que unen la casa con el exterior. Enteramente construida en madera, el montaje de los once módulos y su ensamblaje in situ duró apenas 12 horas.

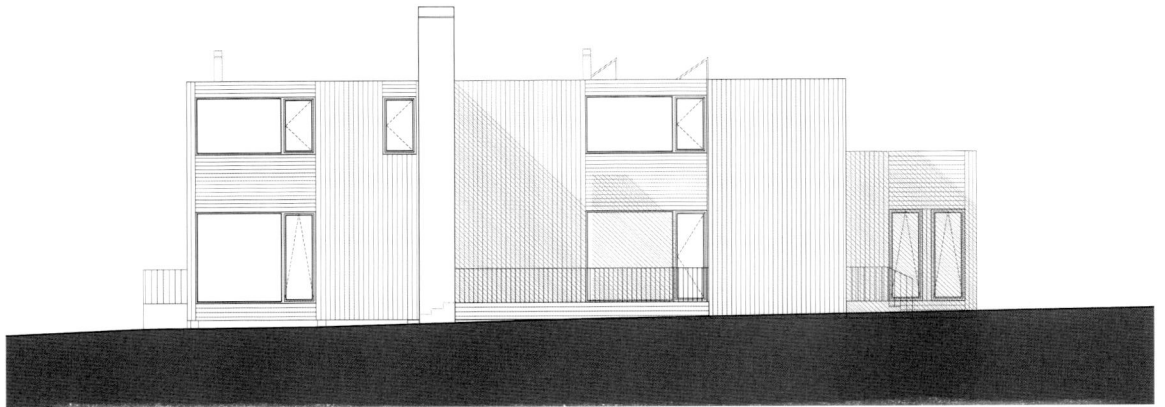

East elevation

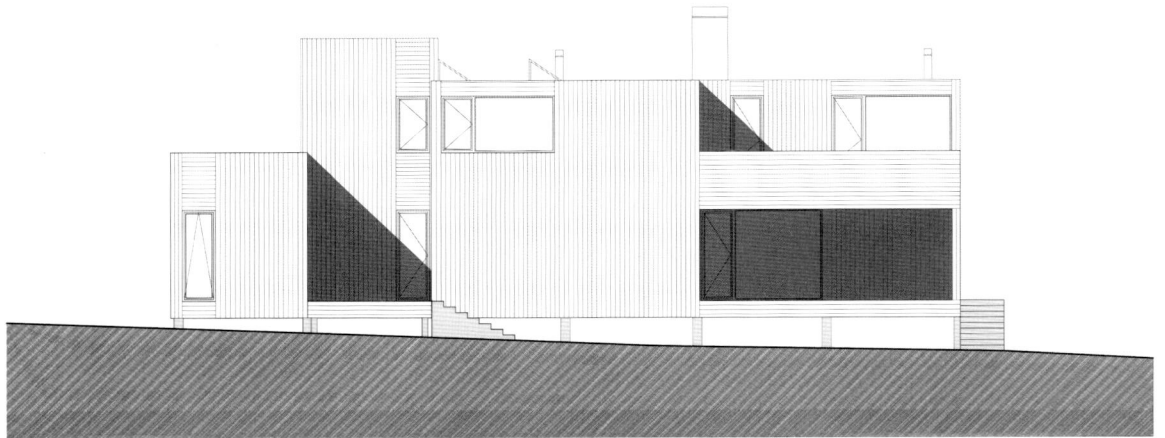

West elevation

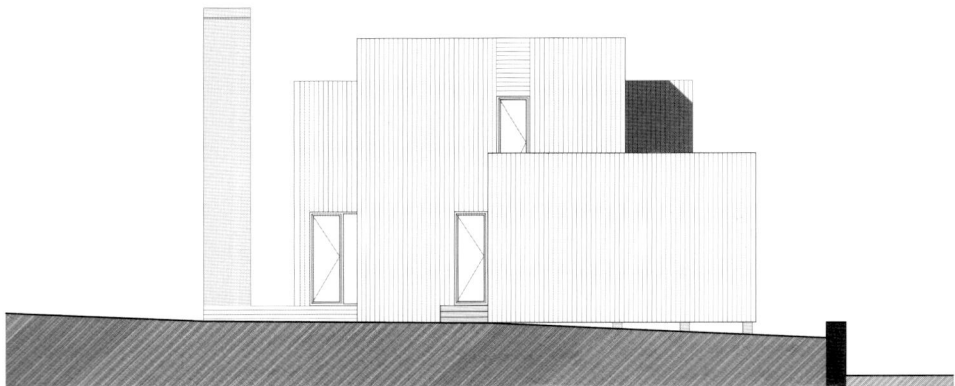

North elevation

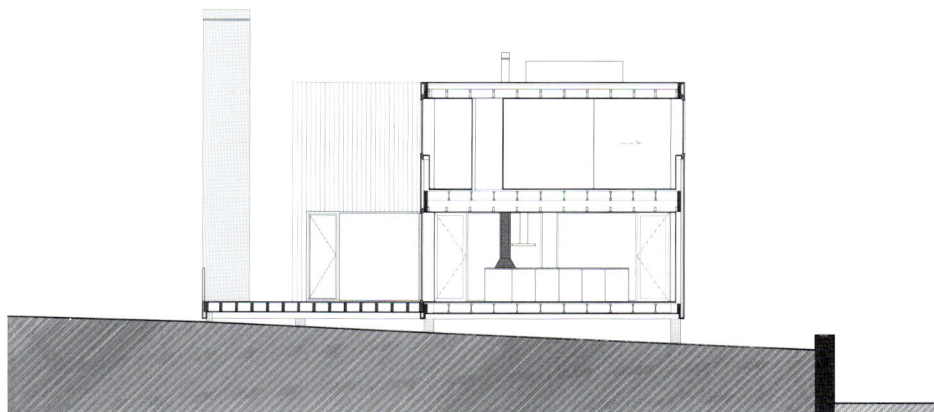

Section

By using a lightweight material such as wood in the structure and cladding of the building, the costs and the environmental impact of this house are reduced.

Al usar un material ligero como la madera en la estructura y revestimientos del edificio, se reducen los costes medioambientales y económicos del proyecto.

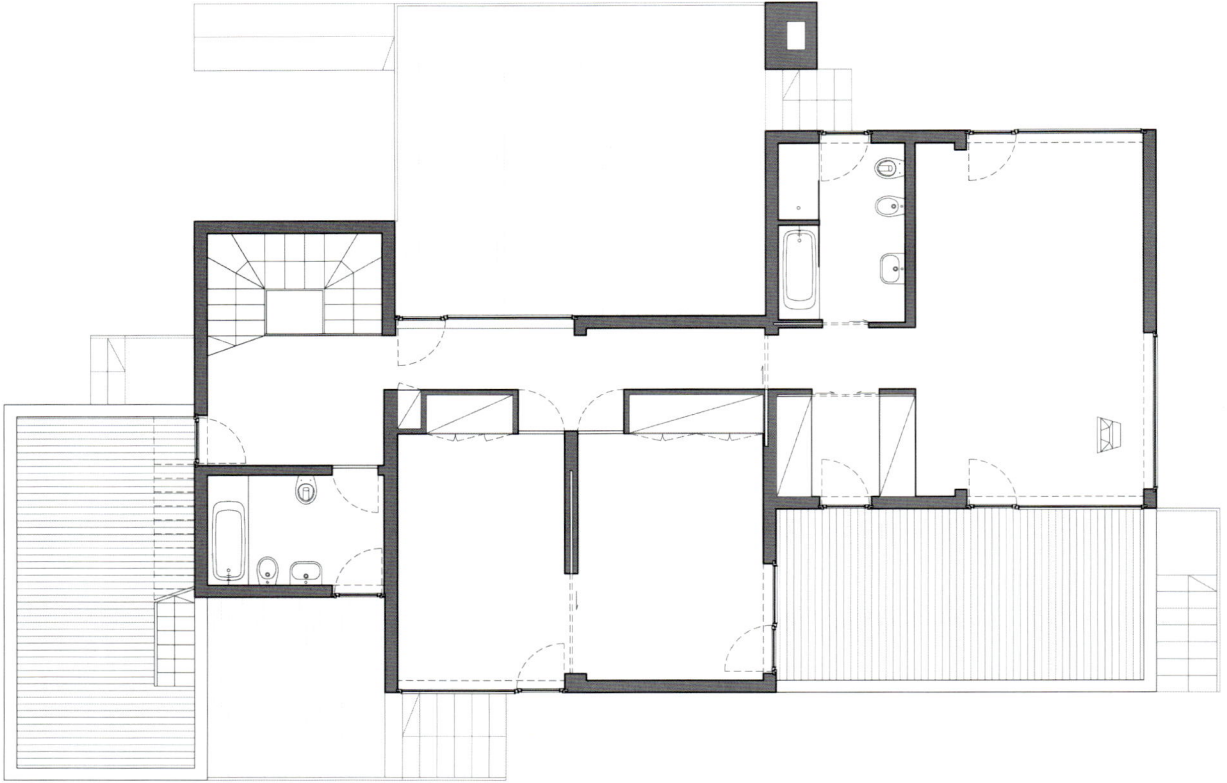

Second floor plan

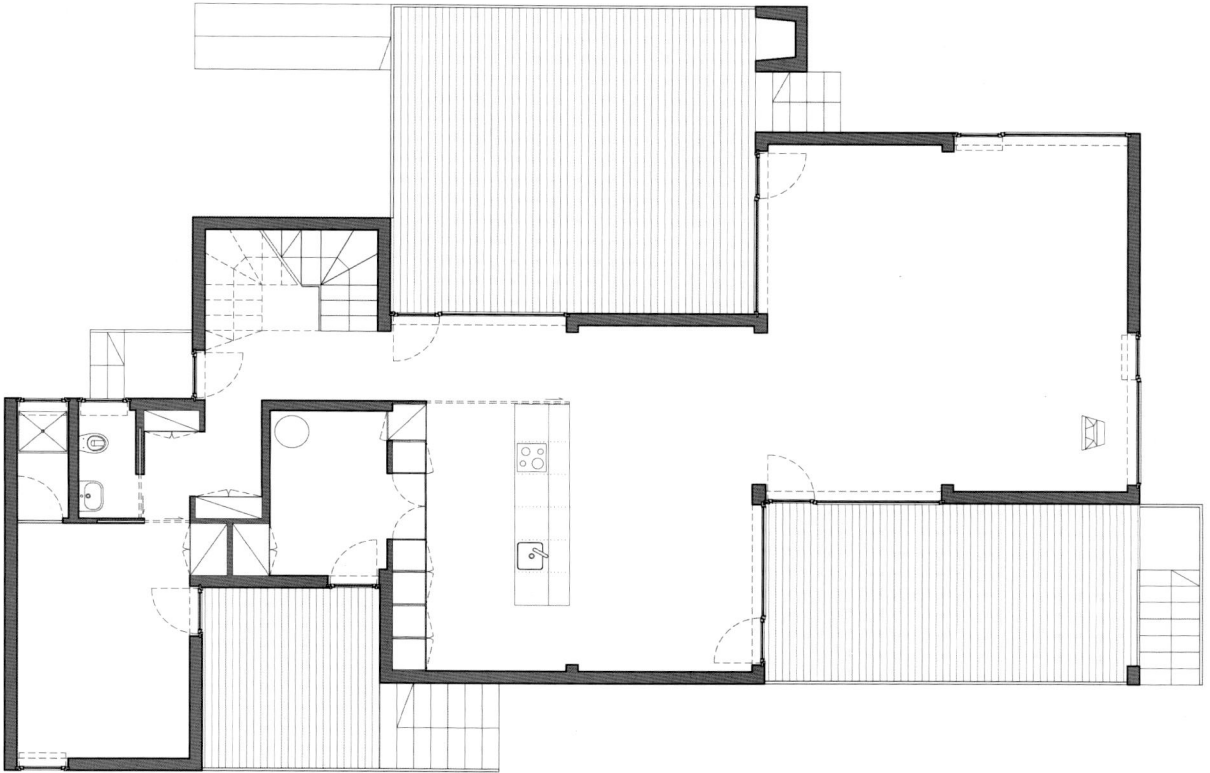

Ground floor plan

This modular system is characteristic for its flexibility, allowing for greater customisation of the design and more possibilities for changes in the future.

El sistema modular usado destaca por su flexibilidad, permitiendo una gran personalización del diseño y la posibilidad de cambio en el futuro.